yes.

She Knows
She's Here

Nicola Schaefer

Published by:

Inclusion Press © 1997

24 Thome Cres.
Toronto, Ontario
Canada M6H 2S5

Printed in
Toronto, Canada
at New Concept

Proceeds from sales will assist the

*Centre for Integrated
Education and Community*

Canadian Cataloguing in Publication Data

Schaefer, Nicola   1939 -

Yes! She knows she's here

Includes Index
ISBN 1-895418-28-3

1. Schaefer, Catherine, 1961 - Health
2. Cerebral palsied - Canada - Biography.
I. Title

RC388.S36 1997   362.1'96836'0092   C97-932169-7

Appreciation

I would like to express my gratitude to the
Manitoba Arts Council for its assistance.

Catherine's complete story, originally published as
"Does She Know She's There"
will be revisited, updated and reissued by
Fitzhenry & Whiteside in 1998

Catherine - surrounded by her friends at 822 Preston
(L. to R. Nicola, Leanne, Darlene, Cath, Marie, Evelyn) - 1986

Yes! She Knows She's Here

Table of Contents

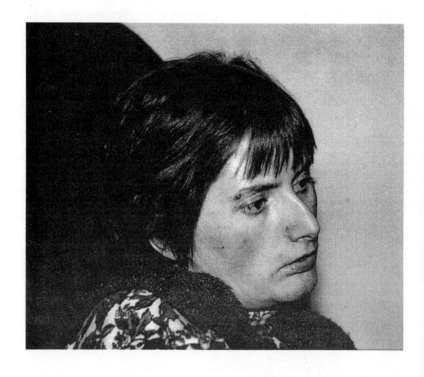

Catherine in a thoughtful mood

Introduction

Many biographies of a person born with a disability have a synopsis on the front flap that starts something like this: "At seven months Catherine was diagnosed with severe and widespread brain damage which would affect her entire neuromuscular system. Her mother was told that Catherine would never walk or talk and would become an increasing burden to her family. She was advised to put her baby in an institution."

The next paragraph, the one designed to hook you on the book, might go: "This is the amazing and heartwarming story of how Catherine's parents refused to accept the grim prognosis and how, through courage, faith and determination, they helped their daughter surmount her awesome disabilities. Now, thirty-five years later, Catherine is happily married and has two healthy children. Having acquired a Ph.D. in anthropology (specializing in the left big toe of prehistoric man), she is Dean of Arts at Gungho University. In her spare time she flies back and forth - yes, she has a pilot's license! - to Equador to volunteer with political refugees."

I enjoy reading such books. We all know, however, that such tragedy-to-triumph transformations rarely occur. It certainly didn't for my daughter Catherine. The first paragraph of this introduction applied to her and to this day (she's thirty-six) she is unable to move much at all, let alone walk, and she has never spoken. Nevertheless, she is a beautiful and fascinating person and I believe her life to date has been equally valid a success story.

In 1978 Fitzhenry & Whiteside (Toronto) published **Does She Know She's There?**, a book I wrote about growing up with Cath, and in 1982 I added to it for an up dated edition. Both Catherine's life and my own got pretty busy after that and I failed until now to continue her story. Fitzhenry & Whiteside are planning to publish Catherine's entire biography - the updated version and this chunk - as a single entity in 1998, but until then Jack and Marsha of Inclusion Press have kindly offered to produce simply this chunk. They believe it stands on its own and might help inspire other families. To put it in context, the following few pages are a distillation of the main book.

Nicola's Story

I grew up in a large, pleasantly chaotic family in southern England. I'm not particularly bright, certainly not an intellectual. I'm relatively outgoing, gregarious and optimistic by nature. I deal with problems mainly by talking about them and hoping they'll disappear. My husband Ted comes from a tightly-knit Mennonite background and grew up in a small southern Manitoba town. He's extremely bright, definitely an intellectual. He's an intensely private person and cautious by nature. He deals with problems by not talking about them and hoping they'll disappear. We met while I was working in a string of struggling cafes in Oxford - my home town - and he was completing his doctoral thesis in the field of nuclear magnetic resonance. We were an unlikely couple but, after I'd emigrated to Canada, decided to marry. Ted by that time had joined the Chemistry Department at the University of Manitoba and, apart from a couple of sabbaticals in England, we've lived in Winnipeg ever since.

We were delighted with our firstborn, Catherine, who was born in July, 1961, but I realized later that almost from the beginning my delight was tempered with disquiet. Even as a neophyte mother I knew that after a few weeks she should be holding her head up, focusing her eyes, reaching out for objects, taking an interest in the world around her. But she did none of these things and seemed to live in the proverbial world of her own. What really frightened me, though, was the amount and quality of her crying. It was a high-pitched, agonized scream, and she would do it for the major part of each day and night. Her record, I masochistically recall, was twenty-one hours non-stop. It was often preceded by a twitch or jerk in her body and was probably, did I but know it, some horrible form of convulsant activity in her brain.

After seven months of little sleep for any of us and an increasing unease on, especially my part, I took her to a child developmental specialist and was given the wretched news that Catherine had severe and widespread brain damage, particularly on the left side, that would drastically affect her physical and intellectual development.

I didn't dispute the doctor's diagnosis - it was almost a relief, in a curious way - but nor did I for an instant take seriously his advice that I institutionalize her. When he looked at her he apparently saw only a clinical mess, a dud that might as well be put away and forgotten about. When I looked at her I saw our beautiful baby daughter who had the need and the right to grow up as normally as possible within the loving circle of her family. Ted agreed, although he didn't have the same innate belief and determination as I did that things would somehow work out okay.

Having discounted other possible causes for Catherine's condition, I accepted the explanation that it was probably the result of an embryo-damaging virus I had, without knowing it, in the first trimester of my pregnancy. So, with Ted's co-operation, I produced our first son, Dominic, almost exactly nine months after Cath's diagnosis. He was the perfect baby, a great tonic for his parents. Three years later our last baby, Benjy, was born. I'd always visualized having four children but a few years later got a dog instead. Far less complicated. The boys prevented their parents, but particularly me, from becoming too zeroed in on Cath. They also pulled their sister along developmentally.

Theories such as infant stimulation, normalization and inclusive education hadn't yet surfaced in the early '60s. Apart from institutional care there was absolutely no assistance either for children with Catherine's kind of difficulties or their parents. Even regular physiotherapy was unavailable because it wasn't considered worth helping children who were intellectually as well as physically disabled. So Cath was at home with me virtually non-stop till she was twelve, when some other parents and I got a school program going.

Her screaming diminished when she was a year or so, although she continued to have numerous brief, twitchy seizures. She began to develop a distinct and charming personality. She was both increasingly aware of her surroundings and responding more often to us, and giving us the sense that she was glad to be alive. She also smiled and laughed more often and had a wicked sense of humour. Sometimes we understood what set her off laughing - if Ted banged his thumb with a hammer, for instance - but she often appeared to enjoy private jokes. We never really knew, nor do we now, how her mind worked,

how much she understood, what she thought, but
we always talked to her in a normal way and
encouraged others to do so.

She had good use of her left arm and hand, of
which to this day she is extremely protective, and
became adept at reaching for some things (Ted's
glasses were a favourite) and pushing away others
(me approaching to clean her teeth wasn't a favourite).
But apart from that, and some spastic kicking with
her legs, she didn't move much. When she was six,
and too long and gangly to carry over my shoulder, I
got her a wheelchair. When she got too big for the
sled Ted had elongated, I had a custom-designed one
built. In other words, we learned to adapt to her
needs. Later, when she was twelve and I found
lugging her upstairs tricky, we restructured our
ground floor to accommodate her.

When Benjy was born we bought a house and I
quickly made friends with other mothers on the
street. Our kids, including Cath, who was viewed
simply as a child with more peculiarities than most,
became almost interchangeable. Our place was
often teeming with the boys' little friends and
between them they discovered innumerable ways to
incorporate Catherine into their play: hauling and
swinging her around on the wooden floors by her
feet, which made her shriek with laughter; piling
cushions on her, which she would bat away with her
left arm; popping balloons inches from her face and,
later, swiveling her around in her wheelchair at high
speed. She really was just part of the gang.

Anxious to avoid the boys feeling resentful towards

Cath due to the different and often constant attention I had to pay her, I made sure they participated in the same activities as their friends, such as Gym and Swim at the Y, Cubs, piano lessons, summer day camp, being naughty, and so on. Ted spent a preponderance of his time in his lab at the university in those days and to ensure that I didn't go dotty through lack of outside stimulus, I embarked on cello lessons. Even though I never achieved much proficiency, I enjoyed myself enormously and it led me into Winnipeg's burgeoning chamber music world, in which I'm still happily involved. As a volunteer and audience member, I should add. We were, as I'd hoped and believed we would be, a fairly typical family.

Periodically in her early years, when I took the boys to England, Catherine spent a few weeks at a time in the St. Amant Centre, a local institution for some 275 children and young adults with disabilities. It never became a home away from home but I did at least feel she was safe there. When we spent a year in London she went with us, of course, as she did in 1971 when we had another sabbatical, this time in Oxford. When in England, the children and I spent much of our time with my mother, Cordelia, and my stepfather, Harry, an actor, in our family cottage in the West Sussex countryside. Nearby were numerous other relations, all, like Mum and Harry, strongly individualistic and, by Winnipeg standards, deeply eccentric. Cath fitted in well.

The local Spastics' Centre (sic) in Oxford offered to have Catherine join its day program three days a week. I'm sure she appreciated the change, and I reveled in having a few hours totally to myself for the first time in ten years (Ted and the boys were working or at school respectively).

When we returned to Winnipeg I screwed up my courage and visited the huge institution for adults with disabilities, 40 miles away, where Cath would have to live should I die or become incapacitated. The experience terrified me into action. I joined forces with a strong and knowledgeable woman I'd recently met through our children (Alice's daughter had seriously incapacitating problems) and, together with three other parents we formed an action group for our kids and the fifty-five or so others in Winnipeg we knew who were living with their families with little or no assistance. Not being as language-conscious then as we are now, we called ourselves *Action for the Dependent Handicapped.* The relevant social services minister literally didn't believe what we told him; he thought that all individuals with significant disabilities lived in institutions. He and his underlings did everything possible to sweep us back under the carpet.

We had to work incredibly hard and be equally persistent to achieve our goal, which was to make the needs of our kids and their families both known and met. It involved endless meetings, writing proposals and briefs, rewriting them, waiting, and somehow keeping ourselves buoyed up. We did succeed in getting our kids' existence acknowledged but then encountered an inventive variety of non-arguments against **doing** anything. However, with help from some enlightened people of influence, we managed to get a life skills program going in a regular elementary school, to which Cath went with enjoyment and where she learned to feed herself with a spoon.

She was becoming a teenager and I became ultra-conscious of helping her look as attractive as possible - dressing her like her peers, giving her nice hair-dos, minimizing her oddities, keeping her chin drool-free, etc. Dominic and Benjy, always good brothers, advised me when necessary ("Face it, Mum, she needs a bra.")

When my book **Does She Know She's There**? came out I discovered a wonderful network of people across Canada and elsewhere who held the same view as I did about Catherine and company: that they were full citizens and deserved to be recognized as such. It was exciting to find myself part of a national movement to redress some of the wrongs being perpetrated upon people who were devalued, both in and out of institutions.

On the local front I met some new activists, too. One was Zana Lutfiyya, who was working in 'the field' and who Ted permitted to move in and tend to Cath when I went to out to town meetings and conferences. Another was David Wetherow, who was to have a profound effect on our lives. It was a whole new era and I started to believe that Catherine had a worthwhile future as an adult.

Now read on.....

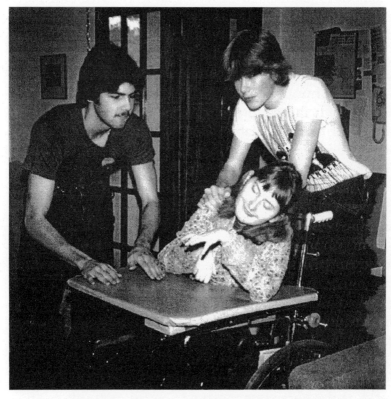

Dominic, Benjy and Catherine (c. 1978)

Yes! She Know She's Here

Nicola Schaefer

It's a handsome house. Old, wood-framed and painted white with a black roof and trim, it has three storeys. It faces a pleasant park where one can enjoy concerts, picnics, celebrations and evening saunters in the summer, and crunchy walks along its paths in winter. It's in a friendly, elm-shaded neighbourhood close to downtown Winnipeg. It's five minutes from where she grew up and it's been Catherine's home since July 18th 1986.

"Is it the one on the corner with the curved path sloping up to the back door," someone asked recently, "the one with the lovely flowers everywhere?"

"That's it, yes. And the path is actually a disguised ramp. I'm glad you were fooled!"

This conversation took me back nearly a decade to when planning began in earnest for Cath's move to her own place. The idea of her living in an apartment with the necessary supports had lurked at the back of my mind for a while but had then been superseded by an even better plan.

A few years previously I was at a conference talking about Catherine's life and had met a charming psychiatrist, Hugh LaFave, who later became the Executive Director of the Canadian Association for Community Living[1] in Toronto and who was a wonderfully fresh force in the movement for change and community living. He told me that my apartment idea reminded him of when he was a medical student. He'd thought how great it would be if a house could be set up that would meet a variety of people's needs. He imagined a friendly, middle-aged couple - maybe retired but still active - living in a third floor self-contained apartment; they would be responsible for the smooth running of the house. Four younger people would have bedrooms on the second floor and the ground floor would be their communal space, with the usual arrangement of sittingroom, dining room and kitchen. Three of these young people would be students, probably in subjects like medicine (that's where Hugh would fit in), psychology and teaching and the fourth person would be someone who had a disability and needed friendship and support to lead a good life. The benefits would include a learning experience for all concerned.

I said I thought it sounded marvelously innovative and that it could work well for a person with less complex inconveniences with which to contend than Cath but felt it wouldn't be the answer for Cath herself. Then, mainly because there was no funding in sight for anyone with her sorts of needs, I forgot about it.

Disappeared

I'd always been grateful for the existence of St. Amant as a place where Cath could go when I took off for England with the boys, but I was never exactly thrilled to leave her there. As the automatic front doors opened and I wheeled her in, her expression seemed to undergo a subtle change. It didn't become anything as specific as unhappy, anxious or displeased but her slightly lowered eyelids and the suspension of her customary arm-flapping suggested quiet resignation, an emotional shutting down. I'd also become increasingly uncomfortable running around talking about community alternatives to institutions and then sheepishly adding that I still made use of just such a place on occasion.

A small but significant occurrence the last time I'd picked her up after going to England proved to be what finally spurred me to action. As I walked down the main hall of her ward I passed an alcove in which a group of about fifteen residents were propped up in or hanging over the edges of their wheelchairs. They were in a semi-circle around a huge colour TV that was showing a steamy scene from a soap opera that looked as though it was probably called "The Doomed and the Dreary." A couple of attendants standing behind the group were watching it but, as I cast my eye over the people in wheelchairs, I noticed that not one of them had their eyes anywhere near the TV. It was utterly irrelevant to them. I went to Cath's room and was surprised to find it empty.

"So you've lost my daughter?" I said to the nurse at the desk. She looked up and smiled.

"Hi, Mrs. Schaefer, good to see you. Now you know we wouldn't do that. She's watching TV. She's been no trouble at all, as usual."

Puzzled, I walked back to the group. I scanned it slowly and, sure enough, there was Cath in the middle, head drooped on her chest, fast asleep. I was horrified to realize that I hadn't seen her the first time, hadn't been able to distinguish her from all the other bored young people in the wheelchair circle.

She had, in a sense, disappeared.

Well, I thought, I don't know how I'm going to do this, but that's the last time Catherine is going to St. Amant. I have to cut that umbilical cord. Maybe I'll just have to give up going to England.

Later I took a deep breath and told my thoughts to our friend David Wetherow, Winnipeg Association for Community Living's Executive Director. He put his arm around me and gave me a big squeeze.

"Good for you," he said, "good for you! We've been wondering when you'd have the courage to do this."

I was taken aback. "You have? And who is we? Who have you been discussing me with?"

"All of us who care about you and Cath. We decided we shouldn't say anything to you, though. It had to be your decision. But now you've made it we'll be there for you. Rest assured, we'll sort out something for Cath next time you go to England."

The Trip to the Rockies

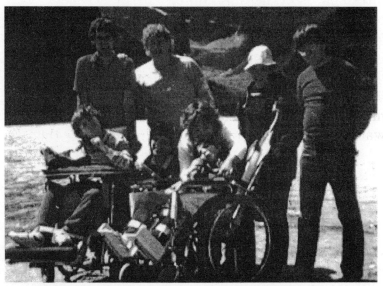

Zana (second from right - back); Jay(right - back)

I got an almost identical reaction from Zana - "God! What a relief you've finally come to that conclusion!" - and from several other friends.

Early in the summer of 1983 I put everyone to the test by announcing that while Dominic was planning to clean buses for the City for most of the summer, Benjy and I wanted to go to England for the month of August.

In 1980 a community residence had opened in Steinbach, Manitoba, a small town near Winnipeg. It was created largely due to the efforts of Martha, a friend of mine who, despite the fact that her daughter had died some years before in the big institution, continued to be active in procuring good alternatives in the community for people with multiple disabilities. Apart from having been forced by the Government to accommodate too many people - six plus two 'respite' beds - the home ranked high in many people's estimation, including mine. Debbie, the house manager, heard that I was looking for a place for Catherine and kindly invited her to stay for the last two weeks of August and Zana came up with an imaginative if scary plan for the first two.

Zana was working for the Manitoba Association for Community Living (ACL Manitoba) at the time and was in charge of its summer holiday program for people with complex disabilities. Cath had, incidentally, been the catalyst for creating the program a year or two before. Zana had funding from various sources but no (building) facility so, with encourage-ment from Dale Kendel, ACL Manitoba's Executive Director, she set about planning for Cath and two other young people in the program. They decided to take a trip to the Rockies.

Although I was intrigued by the idea when I first heard about if I soon developed a daunting list of possible disasters. Cath had camped overnight before but this was different. What if, for instance, despite the carefully planned menus which included loads of fresh fruit, veggies and bran, Catherine's innards clogged up? What if she developed a chest infection that didn't respond to the antibiotic I was sending along? What if a bear took a fancy to her? I decided that the concept of allowing people who have disabilities 'the dignity of risk,' i.e. not over-protecting them, is all very well but only when applied to *other people*. However, as I heard the details of the expedition develop my qualms subsided, somewhat.

There were five assistants accompanying Cath and her two friends - three women, including Zana, and two men. All were at university, studying a variety of subjects that included education, chemistry, psychology and theology. Three of them had experience working with persons who had severe disabilities, four had camping experience and two were certified in First Aid. In addition to this expertise, they all had tremendous enthusiasm about the proposed trip. They spent individual time with the three protagonists of the party and their excited but dubious families and became knowledgeable about their regular routines, habits, medications, diets and preferences. Then they set up meal plans (rough), medication charts (precise) and started working out routes.

Next they rounded up camping gear, mostly borrowed: two tents, air mattresses, sleeping bags, lanterns, cooking equipment, coolers, umbrellas, a daunting box of disposable undergarments, a bike pump for the wheel chairs and a Trivial Pursuit game. Then, when they saw it all massed from wall to wall and ceiling to floor in our dining room, they wondered how they'd ever fit it, plus eight people, into our van and the small car they were taking. But they did, and off they set across the prairies hours after Benjy and I boarded the plane for England.

Apart from a few minor problems common to any such trip, such as burnt food and lost roads, nothing

21

went seriously wrong and eight friends thoroughly
enjoyed a memorable camping holiday together.
Cath brought back with her a photo album of the
jaunt and a diary kept by the assistants. We still
enjoy looking at these books. To give a taste of the
trip here's an extract from an article written later by
Zana:

*Three days later we (the women) joined the
guys in Banff. We camped at Tunnel Mountain,
a beautiful spot. We decided to cut Jasper out of
the trip, spend more time in Banff and return
home via Calgary. This allowed us to adopt a
slower pace and see more of Banff, which is a
lovely town. We strolled around, watching the
other tourists and admiring the Rocky Mountains.
We spent a full day at Lake Louise and managed
to walk halfway around the lake before the path
got too steep to manage the wheelchairs. A
picnic at Coral Creek with a red and white
checked tablecloth; a spaghetti dinner with
homemade sauce and two bottles of wine; the
gondola ride at Sulphur Mountain; shopping
for souvenirs for ourselves and our families -
these are the memories from the Rockies.*

*We drove to Calgary, down from the clean,
crisp mountain air to the muggy prairies.
Mounds of laundry and eight baths later, we all
spruced up and went out to a highly recommended Chinese restaurant. We had a great
time, with cocktails followed by lots of fine food.
As had been the case throughout our trip, we
received excellent and respectful service, with*

the waiters going out of their way to get to know us all and what would please us. After dinner we took a stroll through a beautiful island park in the heart of Calgary and listened to performers at the Folk Festival. The city and park were all lit up and so were we.

All through the holiday we drew double takes and long looks. We welcomed them, especially from children. We would always smile (or smile back) and try to start a conversation. Children wanted to know why some people couldn't walk or talk, and then wanted to know what they could do. Adults were amazed that we were on holiday, all the way from Winnipeg. Fortunately they were so struck by this fact that they forgot to tell us all how wonderful we were for doing this. What we could probably never have explained to them was how much fun we had had on the trip ourselves.

Everyone seemed powerfully affected by the trip to the Rockies but none more so than Jay, one of the men assistants. He was a chemistry student at the beginning of the holiday but by the end of it he had decided to switch to medicine. He wanted to become a neurologist so that he could help people like Cath and her friends. The last I heard he was well on his way.

The Early 1980's

Several significant events occurred in the late '70's and early '80's that were to change the lives of many people with disabilities in Manitoba, including, for the first time, those with complex problems such as Catherine experienced. In the summer of 1979 Dale Kendel, ACL Manitoba's Executive Director, and John Robertson, an enthusiastic and community-spirited journalist, headed a group of people who organized a twenty-six mile Marathon to raise funds for projects in the community to support people with a mental handicap. Some four and a half thousand runners took part and it was immensely exciting. Zana, Cath and I camped overnight in the van where the race started so that we could be up at 5.00 a.m. to be stickers-on of numbers on the competitors' shirts. While the runners ran we had a protracted breakfast at a nearby pancake house and then waited at the finish line (the race was circular) to cheer everyone as they returned. The professionals merely shook off their sweat and checked their time but others, arriving much later, wobbled and weaved their way down the final stretch and collapsed into the welcomers' arms.

The Marathon has continued annually and, as well as raising three and a half million dollars to date, has been a terrific instrument for public awareness.

Says Dale:
The significant impact of the Manitoba

Marathon has been the strategic use of these three and a half million dollars to initiate new concepts (apartment living, smaller community residences, shared accommodation, employment options, etc.) that have now become common place. These concepts, once successfully implemented, have received ongoing provincial Government funding and the designs have been replicated. Apartment living, for instance, started with twenty-nine people and now supports three hundred and eighty individuals throughout Manitoba. Overall, in excess of forty million dollars have been attracted to projects over the last decade and a half, and in total, two hundred and thirty-two projects have been supported, so clearly the Marathon has played an extraordinary role in influencing the services and supports that have been developed in Manitoba.

One year, I recall, I went to the river road down which Cath, Coda (our dog) and I regularly walked, to yell encouragement to the runners at the mid-way point. A middle-aged man plodded grimly past, his mouth open, a bandage holding one knee together. "Doing it for Cath," he managed to croak, "my way of helping." Further on he veered off to the side of the road to pass under a shower someone had thoughtfully rigged up with a garden hose. It was only then that I recognized him as a friend from the Chemistry Department of the University of Manitoba. I felt a twist of guilt but then realized he wouldn't be doing it if he didn't want to and that the Marathon was a way for people to do their bit for the cause if they couldn't become directly involved in peoples' lives.

A New Democratic Party (NDP) Government was returned late in 1981 and an old friend of Alice's and mine, Muriel Smith, a human rights activist of long standing, became the Minister of Community Services two years or so later. She understood the necessity of making it possible for people with disabilities to have decent lives, and one of the first things she did as Minister was to launch what became known as Project Welcome Home. Under the auspices of this plan some two hundred and twenty people would be sprung from the big institution, St. Amant, and another small but isolated institution. Funding would be provided to help an equal number of adults with disabilities move from their parental homes into the wider community. The process was to take about three years and rural areas would be addressed first.

There was chaos at first, rather similar to the scenes one sees on TV when a planeload of food lands amidst thousands of starving people. Many of us had been starved of hope that we would ever see money going towards creating alternative living situations in the community for people both inside institutions and out, rather than being used only for improving institutions or even adding on to old ones.

A confusion of committees was set up to sort out how the whole process would work. This alone took almost a year. There had to be equal representation from community agencies, and relevant civil servants, some of whom had been regurgitated from the bad old days and were neither relevant nor civil. I was reminded of the excruciating time when Alice and I and other members of Action for the Dependent Handicapped had to wrestle with these people when they had no intention of listening to us, let alone doing anything constructive. There was a difference this time, however, due to Muriel's policy and her determination to make it work.

I forget how many committees I was on - at least four - but I seemed to spend much of my life shut up in one of several artificially-lit, stuffy board rooms arguing vociferously and trying to make sense of what someone was diligently writing on the flip chart. Alternately, I was travelling to or from one of the institutions. Teams of pertinent people - the individual concerned, family members if any (very often, sadly, people had no known relatives), social workers, institutional staff, community agencies which could potentially serve the person - were created to plan the resettlement in the community of the people chosen to be sprung.

Like many of my friends, I was on several of these teams as a sort of bi-partisan community advocate. The sense of ear-humming, sweaty horror I'd felt ten years previously, when I went to investigate the big institution, never failed to stun me as I entered the place. And even though we were there to do something positive it was sad and frustrating to know that only a few of the hundreds of men and women in the place would escape to a real life.

The staff members were almost universally pleasant and eager to cooperate but there was a curious attitude

prevalent that the inmates could be divided into two
groups: those who were "ready for the community"
and those who, due to the complexity of their
disabilities, were not. "Mary shouldn't be in here,
she doesn't belong. But Lucy, in that bed over there,
she'll always be with us." How often we heard such
comments. We knew that everyone in the place
could live in the community. They were all ready for
it, providing, of course, that the necessary support
was available. It was more a question of whether
the community was ready to welcome the person.

Looking at the lists of people around whom we
were to plan, it was depressing to see that they were
described mainly in negative terms: "No. 3593, M.,
47, wheelchair, seizures, profoundly retarded;" or,
"No. 4487, F. severe retardation, non-verbal, self-
abusive, violent."' Several people had "wanders"
listed among their non-attributes and a typographical
error on one turned this into "wonders." I'll bet he
wonders, said someone.

I remember on one trip we met a dignified, middle-
aged fellow called Max who shyly told us he dreamed
of living in his own place back in Altona, where he
came from, and that he got angry when people tried
to make him do things like spend the day unscrewing
gadgets and then being told to screw them up again.
"Wheelchair, non-compliant," it said when I checked
the list. Who wouldn't be infuriated under these
circumstances? We began automatically to admire
the spirit of anyone who had "non-compliant" by their
name. Conversely, we suspected that "compliant,"
which was used as a positive adjective, meant

28

squashed spirit.

My desk, in fact a table in Cath's room, became a repository solely for piles of proposals and documents associated with Welcome Home. They spread inexorably down to the floor and thence, after a spell on the fridge, into the dining room. My normal desk stuff - mainly heaps of unanswered mail and an alarming file labelled 'to be dealt with now' and dated two years previously - was moved to a space between the piano and the wall, where at least I couldn't see it.

Usually buried amidst the papers, my typewriter, a comfortable old manual full of dog hair, stayed put. This was because Dominic seemed to be turning into an academic, a breed that has always puzzled me. He was working towards an Honors English degree and periodically, after holing up in his room or at the university for days at a time, would appear white and bleary-eyed with, for instance, an armful of erudite essay on Eliot which had to be typed (by me) and handed in tomorrow. He habitually did this while Cath was watching the late night news and I was ready to drop. My screams of outrage caused her much merriment. My sleep pattern had been the same for years: about six hours a night during the week and terrific lie-ins on the weekend. Now, though, there were even meetings at 9.00 on some Saturday mornings.

I hauled myself out of bed on one such occasion, fed and dressed Cath, felt like passing out at the meeting and returned home more than a little fragile. Ted tried to help. "You look awful," he said and I mustered a glare. "You've been at it for months now but how many people have come out of the institutions? And when is anything going to happen for Cath?"

I'd already tried to explain to him that Welcome Home, after the initial and seemingly endless planning, was concentrating on people from rural areas and only later would those from Winnipeg be helped. Wanting to be alone I traipsed down to the basement to do the laundry.

Even when and if Cath's turn did come, I thought, how would her new living situation be arranged and her continuing support co-ordinated? None of the existing community agencies catered for people with her kinds of needs. God, we'd have to start one. How? Who? Tears of tiredness joined the wash as it churned around. When I got upstairs Ted had left for the lab but there was a vase of roses on the kitchen table. "I worry about you," he said later. As one does, I rallied and carried on. The work was relentless but truly was helping people have a life rather than an existence. That kept me going.

Prairie Housing Co-op

One ray of hope for Catherine was another of the initiatives of the early '80s designed to benefit people with disabilities. This was the founding, in 1982, of a housing co-op in Winnipeg that incorporated a small percentage of people with physical or mental disabilities. It was named Prairie Housing Co-operative and was dreamed up by David Wetherow. As part of his role as ACL Winnipeg's Executive Director, he made himself responsible for inventing new ways for people with disabilities to lead good, well-supported lives. Although she didn't become a member until four years later, he says that Catherine was one of the two people who inspired it. "If it won't work for Cath I'm not interested in pursuing it," he said.

Co-operative (working together) housing has existed for decades in many countries but is a relatively new concept in Canada and only just beginning in the United States. The idea of any co-op is that the members, who buy a membership for a nominal sum, refundable if they leave, collectively rent or buy the house, the factory, the store, or whatever it may be and are collectively responsible for running it. The control and responsibility are democratic - one member, one vote - but the usual practice is for the members to elect a Board of Directors from among themselves. This Board looks after the financial and general management of the co-op (the rents cover the costs and anything extra goes towards an "improvement fund") but the fundamental issues are voted on by the general membership.

Sometimes, if the organization gets too big or time-consuming for the Board to run, a manager is hired but the policy and direction of the co-op always remains in the Board's hands and the Board, in turn, is always responsible to the general membership. As David says in an article about co-op housing in his book **The Whole Community Catalogue**[2]

One of the continuing lessons for members in all kinds of co-ops is that there is no 'them.' Ultimately, all action, or inaction, and all responsibility is 'ours.'

What makes co-op housing attractive for many people, particularly those with low incomes, is that because there's no middle person wanting to make a profit it can provide a decent, afford- able place to live - and there's more likelihood of having friendly neighbours.

How It Works

To illustrate the way Prairie Housing Co-op works, one of its first buys were two pairs of side by side houses a few streets from us. Three of the houses were occupied by typical groups of people: a family of three in one, a family of four in another and a young couple without children in another. All these people agreed, when they joined the co-op and moved in, that they would be friendly and supportive to one another but particularly to the people in the fourth house, two women who were friends and who both had a disability. These women received paid support from a social agency in necessary areas, such as job-training, but were able to rely on their co-op neighbours for help with shopping and similar chores with which they weren't yet familiar. (Not much chance to go shopping in an institution.)

All the members of this four-house cluster spent time in each others' homes just because they enjoyed one another's company, and they shared the chores and pleasures of a communal fenced back garden. Most of the households in this cluster have changed by now but the pattern is the same.

David and I often found ourselves at the same meetings to do with Project Welcome Home. After one of them, about a year after my attack of the miseries, I unburdened myself to him concerning Cath's future and where she'd eventually live. He suggested that I start doing what I'd been encouraging other parents to do for their children when I'd spent time with them in the course of Welcome Home: dream, he said, dream about the best possible living arrangement for her. There were many factors in Cath's favour at the moment, he added. One, Prairie Housing Co-op, with invaluable assistance from a fellow named Al Charr in the Government's Department of Co-operative Development, was running smoothly and now had several clusters of housing similar to the one near us, so Cath could link into the co-op as he, David, had always intended. Two, Welcome Home had for some time been providing funding for Winnipeg residents who needed to move away from their parental homes or who were in danger of being institutionalized due to family problems. Three, the Government was making renovation grants available to groups of five people or more, one of whom had a disability, who wanted to set up house together.

Serious Dreaming

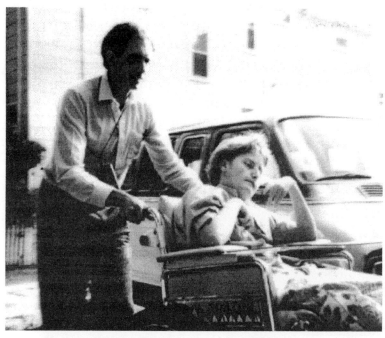

David Wetherow and Catherine

I knew all this, of course, because as well as being involved in many aspects of Welcome Home I was also a Board member of ACL Winnipeg and had consequently been in on Prairie Housing Co-op since its inception. What David said made sense. I should start dreaming for Catherine. I was reluctant at first to take him up on the suggestion, however; I think I saw it as taking advantage of being part of the system. But when he added that the money wouldn't last much longer so it might be now or never,

I went home and embarked on some serious dreaming.

It was knowing about the renovation grants for groups of five people or more that reminded me of Hugh Lafave's idea when he was a medical student, of living in a house with a diverse group of people, one of whom would need support. A house, I thought, why not?

Two of the most seriously negative aspects of having significant disabilities, particularly if one has trouble communicating, are the propensity for loneliness and the likelihood of having in one's life only people who are paid to be there. It seemed to me that Catherine might be prone to these problems if she lived in an apartment with shift staff, however hard we tried to build in supports. David, in another part of his article on co-op housing, notes the following:

> *Another pattern in many residential services (including supported apartment living arrangements) is that people often continue to live in isolation from the surrounding community. My office is in an apartment building (about one hundred units) where ten people with physical disabilities live in their own apartments and share an attendant care system. We couldn't live in closer proximity if we tried, yet there is virtually no interaction between these ten young people and the other tenants in the building. Independent but isolated. Why is that?*

> *The fact is that there is no 'community' in that building, even for the ninety plus people without disabilities. There is nothing about the way the building is organized that brings us*

> *together. Since we have no work to do together,*
> *ordinary shyness, plus the fear that people*
> *experience in connection with disability, keeps*
> *us strangers to each other.*

Catherine had grown up in an ordinary house in a
friendly neighbourhood and from babyhood on had
always been as widely recognized, accepted and
liked for who she was as any other child, including
her brothers. Rather than suddenly finding herself
in an apartment, wouldn't she be more comfortable
in a setting similar to that in which she'd always
been? And maybe with, instead of her family, a
group of friends more or less her age?

But what friends?

Since 1979 Cath and I had been connected with
Winnipeg's l'Arche community. L'Arche, the French
word for the Ark, is an international federation of
intentional communities, varying in size, in which
men and women who have a disability, and their
assistants, live, work and share their lives together.
The assistants are never known as staff; they get
board and room and what amounts to pocket money.
Winnipeg's community consists of twenty-five
people with disabilities. They and the assistants live
in houses, duplexes or apartments all within a few
miles of each other. Jean Vanier, a visionary Canadian
philosopher and theologian, started the first community in a village in France in 1964 and there are now

some hundred communities in thirty countries all over the world, including several in England. Many of the assistants in Winnipeg's community have been and are from Manitoba but over the years many have come from other countries. I'm pleased to have been instrumental for importing three so far. Assistants stay in a community sometimes for weeks and sometimes for years. Whichever the case the experience seems to have a profound effect on them; a writer acquaintance of mine here spent a summer in our community when she was a teenager and is still, years later, quite connected, writing articles for and about l'Arche and retreating to the original community in France when life overwhelms her.

I was invited onto the Board a couple of years after Cath and I became friends of l'Arche. At a retreat soon after (a weekend in a Benedictine nunnery) for Board members and assistants, I was asked what I thought I brought to l'Arche. I couldn't think of anything. I felt I got far more from the people, both with and without a disability, than I could ever give. In the end I looked at my daughter and said, "Catherine." I was gratified to find that others agreed with me; in a community where vulnerability is virtually a plus, because of what one can learn from those who are vulnerable (including one's own vulnerability and fragility), she ranks high. L'Arches across Canada are beginning to welcome people with more severe disabilities to live in their communities and when it happens in Winnipeg I'll know Cath has played a part in the move.

In 1985, as in other years, I flew all over Canada

and the United States, talking at conferences about growing up with Catherine.

I enjoyed all these trips but the one that gave me the most joy and satisfaction was in the company of Cath herself. We went as part of l'Arche Winnipeg to spend a weekend in Edmonton with the l'Arche communities from that city, Calgary and Illinois. There were about forty-five of us, including those with a disability, the assistants who lived with them, Board members and friends. We went by train, nineteen hours each way, and a journey I'd rather dreaded (trains are not designed with users of wheelchairs in mind) proved to be a really positive and enjoyable experience. Everybody in one way or another pitched in to help Cath; everybody helped everybody, in fact, and the same was true of the whole weekend. It underlined for me the absolute necessity of assisting people with disabilities to create around themselves a network of steadfast friends.

In considering friends who might like to share Cath's house, the first who came to mind were Lauchie and Evelyn, former l'Arche assistants who had recently moved out of the community with their small daughter, Marie. They'd be perfect, I thought, a settled, cheerful family. Evelyn was a Montessori teacher but at the moment was mostly at home with Marie, and Lauchie was training to be a nurse. They would lend an air of stability and warmth to the household and, most important, they liked Catherine.

I told them the plan for the house and then tenta-tively asked if they might be interested in being part of it. I had a lengthy speech prepared about how I understood why they couldn't take me up on such a wild idea and was literally speechless when they immediately said yes, how soon? It transpired that they were dissatisfied with their living situation and missed being part of the give and take of a larger household.

David was once again the recipient of my thoughts about a house. " Go for it," he said, "look for a house and report back when you've found one you think would be suitable." Prairie Housing would then give it the once-over, as would people from the Canada Mortgage and Housing Corporation, who were helping Prairie Housing to obtain low interest mortgages. A small group of architects and city planners (friends of the Association for Community Living - Winnipeg) would also want to see the house because they would be the people designing renovations and dealing with licensing and other bureaucratic necessities.

Cath and friends in the l'Arche Walkathon - 1995 (10 Km)

Looking for the House

In looking for a house there were several considerations: it had to be within easy cycling distance of Lauchie's hospital, close to a nursery school for Marie, not too far from us and in a friendly neighbourhood. After several false starts I found a house that fulfilled these requirements and Lauchie and Evelyn and I went to nose around in it, as did the fellows from DSI (the group of planners).

There was a groundfloor apartment, two smaller ones on the second floor and a fourth on the top floor. With a bit of imagination we could visualize the groundfloor becoming a comfortable living space for Cath and two room mates. There was a huge kitchen with plenty of space for a table and six chairs, a good-sized sittingroom, a bedroom and bathroom which would be for Cath's room-mates, and a diningroom which could be transformed into Cath's bedroom and washing facilities.

In addition, there was a small room by the laundry room in the basement, plus a bathroom. Because Lauchie and Evelyn needed a larger space than any one of the upstairs apartments provided, we figured we could rearrange the latter into one large apartment for them and still have room for a small bachelor apartment.

As well as being rearrangeable inside, the house was very attractive on the outside: with a front porch and, above that, a balcony on the second floor, and a nice front garden and lawn surrounded by lilac and other bushes, it looked like what it originally was

- a large middle-class family home. In the park immediately opposite the house was a playground (perfect for Marie) that included a water slide down which children were happily shrieking.

Reflecting the multi-generational nature of the neighbourhood, next to the playground was a green on which a number of elderly people in hats were bowling away the afternoon. Several of our friends lived a stone's throw away from the house, including Chris and Nancy Dafoe, who had returned to Winnipeg after fifteen years in Vancouver. At the other end of the block was a street I knew well because it had some my favourite stores, with names like Prairie Sky Books, Tall Grass Prairie Bakery, The Green Earth Environment Store and Harvest Collective. Close by, too, was Impressions Café (where Benjy often worked). Also only a block away from the house was Portage Avenue, one of Winnipeg's main streets, so it would be easy for people who didn't have cars to get to the house by bus.

That summer, 1985, while I was involved in Prairie Housing's acquisition of the house, Dominic carried out a threat of longstanding and, with a university friend, moved into an apartment in an old block in an unfashionably grotty part of town. "Why you guys wanna move in here?" asked the caretaker suspiciously, as a cop car burned round the corner to deal with a fight in the back lane. "Because we're poor," they said. Dominic was finishing off his degree and cleaning buses for the City just often enough to pay his rent. Most of the time, though, he was working for a small advertising firm that put out, amongst other things, a sort of "What's on in Winnipeg?" magazine. He wore a suit (his father's, dating from the '50s and considered very smart by his contemporaries) and tie and had a pocket full of company cards with his name and 'advertising consultant' on them. Part of the job, as might be inferred from this information, was flogging ad space in the magazine but he was also writing the odd - very odd, he said - article and learning the art of putting a periodical together.

He was also learning, of course, the art of living independently but, in the tradition of sons leaving home, he appeared every few days for a shower and a meal and use of the washing machine. We loved seeing him, even though the house became increasingly denuded as he staggered out to his fifteenth-hand car after each visit with anything he could persuade us we no longer wanted. I drew the line at the sofa.

The idea of leaving the nest seemed to be catching. Even Benjy was talking about moving out when he finished high-school at the University of Winnipeg Collegiate. He was always clever at inventing jobs for himself during school breaks and outdid himself this year. For the last four springs Winnipeg had been plagued by inchworms, which appeared just after the leaves did and gobbled them up, leaving naked trees and a revolting mess on the sidewalks and roads. So, to trap the moths, which hatched in the ground and crawled up the trees in the fall to lay their eggs, Benjy went round the neighbourhood ringing trees with a band of a gluey substance called Tanglefoot - stuff that became ubiquitous around our place and could also have been called Tanglefinger,

Tanglehair, TangleTed (which irritated him) and
Tangledog. However, he did good business. When he
returned to school I had to deal with many a cryptic
phone call, e.g. "Is the worm man still ringing?" or
"Can I speak to the worm-glue guy?" These days,
when young men come round in the spring asking if we
want our trees banded, I think of my entrepreneur son.

A Place of Her Own

Like other adults with a disability in Canada,
when Catherine turned eighteen she started receiving
a social allowance cheque which in theory covered
her living expenses. Since until then she'd never
had anything more than the family allowance that
parents receive for all children, $350 a month
seemed like a bonus and I spent the first cheque on
getting my teeth fixed. If she was eventually to
move into her own place, however, this income would
barely cover her rent and food, let alone her care.

Under Welcome Home, funding was to be provided
to assist Catherine and others with severe disabilities
in new living arrangements on an ongoing basis. It
had to go through a Government-approved agency
and, as I've already indicated, none existed. As with
Prairie Housing, it was David, having observed that
part of ACL Winnipeg's mandate was to provide
creative alternatives for people with Cath's kinds of
needs, who invented the necessary agency.

We called it l'Avenir Community Co-operative,
l'Avenir being the French word for *'the future, that
which is to come.'* The co-op started in a tiny way in

1983 around Catherine and a young man named Arnold who had had to spend years in the big institution and whose family desperately wanted him out. As anyone who has started a new organization knows, it takes a huge amount of planning before anything much happens . So it was with l'Avenir but when it came time for Arnold and Catherine and several other people to move to new abodes everything was in place, including our first general manager, Cindy. Cindy and her husband had recently spent two years with CUSO (Canadian University Service Overseas) in Africa and Cindy had experience working with people who had complex disabilities. We couldn't have found a better person to help l'Avenir grow once David had brought it into being; calm and capable, she was also clever at making good use of limited resources, a skill she'd picked up in Africa.

Very often, in fact usually, a person with a disability has his or her housing and other needs met by a single agency. This is dangerous; I've known several people who have been booted out of an agency because of "difficult," i.e. probably angry and frustrated, behaviour and have lost both their housing and service provider at once. David recognized this and intentionally created Prairie Housing Co-op and l'Avenir as separate entities. To offer my daughter once again as an example, this means that if for some reason she leaves Prairie Housing and lives in other accommodation, she'll still be a member of l'Avenir and have help with other aspects of her life. Conversely, if she finds a better support agency than l'Avenir she can still live in her house with Prairie Housing.

l'Avenir Community Co-operative

The **l'Avenir Community Co-operative**'s stated purpose is: *"to provide the supports which will enable people with mental and/or physical disabilities to live with dignity, fulfillment and security."*

Our goals are:

- *to help members create for themselves meaningful lifestyles that are focused on relationships*
- *to respond creatively to the needs and wishes of members*
- *to enable our members to explore the risks and rewards of life's full spectrum*
- *to support families by addressing their concerns for the lifelong needs of their sons and daughters.*

We are:

- *a small community of members, their families and networks (friends and support staff) living throughout Winnipeg*
- *an agency that supports those members in their homes and places of work and leisure*
- *an agency committed to responding to its members' different and evolving needs*
- *a co-op in which the direction of the agency is determined by the people served*
- *an agency committed to supporting people with significant and challenging disabilities*
- *staff who share the lives and homes of its members*
- *staff who provide assistance for the members and also facilitate friendships for the members*
- *not buildings or property, but PEOPLE.*

46

Most of the points are self-explanatory; I hope they are, anyway, since we spent a long weekend concocting the brochure from which they come. Some I could elaborate upon, however. "To help members create meaningful lifestyles that are focused on relationships," for instance. Good governments, good agencies, good staff all tend by their nature to come and go, so one has to rely ultimately not on these official entities but on friends. I can confidently say that should I disappear right now, Catherine has a network of real friends who would look out for her. We try to make this a reality for all our members. "An agency that supports those members in their homes and places of work and leisure" and "a co-op in which the direction of the agency is determined by the people served." These, I think, are the aspects of our agency that make l'Avenir unusual.

First, people with disabilities, especially those whose disabilities are complex, often have staff who come in on a shift basis. We feel that a home shared by the member and primary support staff is more likely to be what one might call a real home. We may not always follow this direction but at the moment it seems to work for at least some of our members. Second, most similar agencies have a couple of parents on the Board but the direction often stems from people who are simply interested. Our Board, on the other hand, consists almost entirely of the members themselves, plus family members or close friends.

To continue being technical for a moment (I'm constantly being asked how l'Avenir works so I may as well give at least the framework), the number of people served by our agency has fluctuated over the years but we've found that if we try to assist more than twenty people we're in danger of burning out our Manager. The salaries for our Manager and half-time Assistant Manager come from a percentage of the members' social allowance. That is, Cath uses part of her income to pay l'Avenir to manage the supports and services she needs. We usually have about sixty people on the payroll, some who live with and are responsible to our members and others who work for them on a part time or respite basis.

Cath - reflecting on the decade?

Nicola Schaefer

Red River Community College

It's a good thing that, when I wrote in **Does She Know She's There?**[3] in 1982 that there might in a year's time be a program for a small number of people with severe disabilities at the University of Winnipeg, I preceded it with "though I say this with the utmost caution." The program did get started but not until a year later than planned, in the fall of '84, and not at the University. I was never quite sure what went wrong but I suspect that both internal politics, i.e. the University, and external, i.e. the provincial Government, were involved and that one of the main problems was funding. I'll always regret it. The University was an ideal place from our point of view; it was central, a short walk from the Y, where Cath and the other three participants could have swum regularly; it had several communal gathering places like cafeterias; there were often free concerts or films at lunchtime; a number of the professors - some of them friends of mine - were dead keen to see it work; the general attitude of the student body was accepting of people who were atypical in one way or another; and finally, I knew from Dominic and Benjy that probably the most important activity at the University was not, as one might think, attending lectures on philosophy, science and so on, but *hanging out*. And it was while people were hanging out, in cafeterias, in the gym, in the bookstore, at special-interest meetings and in the hallways, that Cath and company, with help, would have the best chance of interacting with the regular students and making friends.

If the University of Winnipeg missed the opportunity of having an interesting group of students in its midst, Red River Community College did not. Red River is a huge educational institution that grew out of the community college movement of the sixties. A couple of the senior people there heard of our proposed project and became excited about it. The result was that, after months of intense planning on the part of David and his staff, the Government Department of Education and Red River, Cath and three other young women (as it happens) went to college.

The co-ordinator, who we found but whose salary was paid by the Department of Education via Red River, was a sparkly young woman called Sandee, who had become involved as a teenage volunteer with people with disabilities. She had worked in the summer program at the Y where Cath had been years before and was also one of the assistants who had been on the Rockies camping trip. Catherine and the other students each had a program designed around her individual strengths and needs. Four eager young women, whose salaries were paid partly by a government grant, were hired as 'facilitators.'

Our gang didn't go round in a clump but, like the other students, did their own thing and met up for lunch or an outing. Cath, for example, as well as other activities, went swimming three times a week - a long ride into town in the hired van for which the project had a grant - and had her daily physio alongside other students exercising in the gym.

Her facilitator evolved a neat trick in the gym: she could get Cath out of her wheelchair and onto the mat by herself but, knowing Cath's penchant for dark hairy men, suggested quietly to her that she point to someone she fancied lifting her out that day. Cath would point, or seem to point, at some young man pumping iron and looking strong and masculine and Cath's friend would then ask him if he could help Cath. The young man, even though he might initially find this somewhat alarming, would invariably comply. Two gains were made; Catherine would emit a shout of pleasure at having her day made in this way and the fellow learned that she wouldn't snap in half when he lifted her and stretched her out on the floor. He also learned that if a streak of drool landed on him in the process it could be kleenexed off with no permanent damage to him.

We realized that the regular students at Red River might be puzzled to see four admittedly unusual people at the college, so a few of us, including a representative from the student council and Cindy, who found herself deeply involved on l'Avenir's behalf, sat down and wrote an explanatory pamphlet in a question and answer format. Who are these people? Why are they here? What can they learn? How can we be supportive? etc. It was pleasing to meet people outside the college and have them tell me, when they discovered I was Catherine's mother, that they thought it was a great idea to have people with disabilities incorporated into the place. Some of the teachers were far from enthusiastic at first ("they should be in a special class somewhere") but most of them eventually realized that having our gang wheelchairing or loping around was, if nothing else, consciousness-raising.

I was grateful that the college program was running smoothly when negotiations around Cath's house got underway. I became involved in one way or another with the house on an almost daily basis and wouldn't have been able to cope had Cath been at home.

822 Preston
(under construction)

Renovations

822 Preston
(front of the house)

Once Catherine's house had been officially bought
by Prairie Housing Co-op, I started lobbying to have
a neighbourhood bunch of house-fixers hired to do
the renovations. They were a good gathering of men
and women, some of whom I already knew, who were
part of a Christian association of families living in
the area who were known as the Grain of Wheat
community. Many came from a Mennonite background and wanted to give something more to the
wider community than their mere presence. Jake,

the community's leader, and his wife and their two sons lived just behind Cath's house and when I took Cath over to meet him and explained the concept of her house he became increasingly interested and keen to take on the job.

My lobbying was successful and work started late in the fall. Stan, one of DSI's architects (the planning group working with Winnipeg's ACL), had done a brilliant job of rearranging the inside of the house on paper but Jake and his mates encountered myriad difficulties in practice. I suppose this happens often but it made me feel guilty when, enthusiasm personified, I dropped by to see how things were going and was met with tales of woe and some fairly unchristian comments and even language.

The worse the problems the more exotic the cookies I made for the team but my discomfort was never quite expunged. Overall, though, the building went according to plan and Jake said how pleased they all were to be working on a house that was designed for someone who would bring an unusual 'gift' to the neighbourhood. He later, incidentally, started Winnipeg's branch of Habitat for Humanity and said that Catherine was one of his inspirations.

I was particularly pleased to see the diningroom being transformed into Cath's bedroom, in the design of which she and I had participated. I was also delighted with Stan's imaginative plan for the ramp up to the back door, which was the one Cath would use. Rather than going straight up, it curved round from the back lane and had a corresponding terraced garden area on either side.

The day finally arrived when, in the spring of '86, the ramp was finished and I was able to push Cath up it and into the house. She'd been in before but we'd had to haul her bumpily up the original steps and go in backwards. What had been a minimal back porch was now a sturdy wooden deck and inside the new main entrance was a room that was to house a Jacuzzi. This room led to the kitchen and the rest of the ground floor.

Due to lack of space I'd had to resign myself to being unable to transfer Cath's big bathtub from our house and to settle instead for a shower area which she'd use in a chair designed for the purpose. The Jacuzzi was David's idea. Not only, he said, would Catherine love being in it - relaxing and warm and bubbly, it might even de-stiffen her somewhat - but other people in the house and their friends would like it too. And not everyone can say, "Come over to our place for a Jacuzzi party!" I tried, but failed, to get a grant for the Jacuzzi on the grounds that it was necessary for Cath's well-being, so Ted and I bought it as a present for the household. It has proved to be worth every penny of its cost.

There are several photos in her album of Cath in her prospective living quarters at different stages of their development. She's looking baffled in most of them, as well she might, or studying her left hand closely. Although we explained what was going on, I'm fairly certain that as far as she was concerned, being in the house held the delicious possibility of someone falling off a ladder, which happened on her first visit, but not that this strange, sawdusty, furnitureless place might become her home. There are also pictures of her and Benjy - he and Dominic were often around - and of her and her friends from Red River when they dropped by as part of an outing.

Finding Room-Mates

The house and its intended use created intense interest on the part of many people. One of them was Colleen, who had taken over from Debbie as manager of the community residence in Steinbach where Cath had stayed after the Rockies trip. Cath had enjoyed subsequent visits there when I was out of town and Colleen had became a good friend. She was returning to Winnipeg to take a Masters degree in business administration and asked to look at the house. By the end of the tour, and having met Lauchie and Evelyn, she decided she'd like to move into the bachelor apartment.

"That's fine," said Ted when I told him, "all very nice. But who's actually going to live with Cath?"

It wasn't the first time he'd asked this reasonable but to me annoying question. Based on nothing but instinct and faith, I simply knew that the right people would turn up at the right time. I tried to justify and amplify up this misty belief by saying that many people I knew lived with men and women who had disabilities, in l'Arche for instance.

"But the people in l'Arche can walk -"

"And run away," I countered, "Cath's never done that."

Ted sighed. "I just can't imagine anyone willing to do all the messy stuff and all that lifting."

"We'll find someone, don't worry."

"Hmm."

"Cynic."

"Realist."

Ted's apprehension was, I guess, understandable. He couldn't believe that our love for Catherine, which superseded the difficulties she engendered, could be felt by anyone else. I agreed in the sense that nobody else would ever love her in the same way that we as her parents did, but I did believe that she had intangible qualities that attracted people to her. Not being with her as much as I was, and especially when other people were around, he didn't have the opportunity to see that she was not only readily accepted as who she was but also actively liked.

The house would be ready for occupation in about three months. It was time to put my belief into action and begin a search for our daughter's room-mates. My first step was to ask likely candidates from my circle of friends and then, if they weren't interested themselves I asked them to think of people they knew who might be. Benjy immediately produced two charming young couples but although they were sympathetic to the idea we all agreed that neither of them was ready to take on such a commitment. One of the couples, too, was on a grim-sounding diet which seemed to consist entirely of brown rice, which Benjy and I didn't think Cath would appreciate.

Next I typed a dozen announcements:

My name is Catherine Schaefer. I'm 25 years old and attend Red River Community College 5 days a week. I have disabilities, so I appreciate assistance in remaining an integral part of my community.

I'm a member of Prairie Housing Co-op, which recently bought a large house overlooking Vimy Ridge Park. It's being transformed into 3 apartments. One will be occupied by a couple with a 3 year old daughter, and another by a single woman. I shall be moving into the first floor apartment in mid-July 1986 and am looking for a friendly, outgoing couple to share my quarters in return for assistance - including lifting.

I can offer free rent, a monthly stipend and time off. If you are interested, please call (then I put my name and number.)

I pasted a recent photo of Cath atop each one and then put the finished products in places where I thought likely respondents would see them.

And that was how we found Darlene, who ended up living with Catherine for two years and who is intricately involved in her life and ours to this day. She phoned, having seen the ad in the Mennonite Central Committee office. She'd just returned from a year of volunteer work in Jamaica with that organization, teaching children who were deaf or hearing impaired. She was now going back to university to complete an education degree that she'd started before going to Jamaica. I was hesitant even to meet her, because I reckoned that living with Cath was a two-person business. However, she insisted on coming round and my first sight of her was a tall, ginger-mopped, vivacious young woman chatting with Benjy on the front porch. A few minutes later Cath came home and Benjy and I watched a shy but definite friendship being struck. She's the one, Mum, he said later, she's just right for Cath. Get her!

Darlene wrote recently:

I remember meeting the Schaefer clan. This was not an ordinary household. I should have known from my phone conversation with Nicola and by her comment about how this job wouldn't work for me if I didn't have a husband or "bloke." Liking the idea of getting a job and a home all in one go, I persuaded her to let me meet her and Catherine. When I got to the house Nicola wasn't there; it seemed she had forgotten about our

*appointment and had gone grocery shopping. So
instead I was greeted by a tall blond guy who was
dressed in a towel. He offered me a glass of orange
juice and we sat in the front porch discussing our
respective lives. Nicola arrived shortly after and
proceeded to make tea and offer me a cup. Not
knowing that it was "English" tea, i.e. disgustingly
strong, I declined milk and sugar. Wanting to be
polite and make a good impression I suffered
through it and then Catherine finally arrived. I
discovered quickly that Cath doesn't communicate
through speech but we got along just fine. By the
end of my three hour visit Cath, Nicola and I
decided that we liked each other and I left seriously
thinking about the possibility of living with Cath.*

Darlene told me later that she pretty well made
up her mind after that first meeting but very sensibly
didn't make a commitment until she'd told her family
and friends and gotten their support. Then it was a
matter of figuring out how it could work. Luckily, a
friend of hers, Leanne - bouncy, blond and immensely
entertaining - appeared on the scene and said she'd
like to join Darlene in this venture and could she
have the little room and bathroom in the basement
of the house? The girls had shared an apartment
before, so it seemed like a good arrangement.
Darlene would be Cath's primary support person
and Leanne, who was studying for a theology degree,
would pay nominal rent and help out in return.

Once everything was agreed upon and Darlene
had discussed the financial end of things with Cindy

at l'Avenir, Darlene spent many hours with Cath and myself, watching me attend to Cath's physical care and then having a go herself. She and I also simply talked and laughed a lot and I was pleased to discover that she was a strong and perceptive woman who wasn't scared to give me her point of view if it differed from mine. As was to be expected, it took Catherine longer to be comfortable with Darlene and vice versa but as I increasingly left them alone together their relationship developed.

Daft Regulations

At the house, renovations were winding up but because it was now classed as a multi-family dwelling there were endless complications which no-one had anticipated. Some of the regulations that cropped up were reasonable and involved being able to exit the house in the case of fire but others were completely daft. For example, an empty storage room in the basement had to have a sprung steel door instead of the original wooden one. Eventually we were able to say good-bye to the posse of Government and City inspectors and also to Jake and his colleagues, though the latter continued to be helpful and friendly towards the household in the years to come.

Then Darlene and Leanne and I between us roped in some twenty friends and day after day, to the accompaniment of loud reggae music on Darlene's ghetto blaster, we scraped and scrubbed and painted like mad. Lauchie and Evelyn and Colleen were similarly occupied upstairs and we'd get together and have huge picnics on whatever clean floor space we could find. One day I walked into the kitchen with a fresh supply of beer and nibbles and found Zana on her knees chipping away at the old linoleum and another couple of friends sloshing paint on the walls. Dominic was painting the hallway and Darlene and Leanne were in the sittingroom shouting to each other over the music as they wobbled around on step ladders and painted around the windows. My God, I thought, it's really happening, Cath is actually going to move in here!

Darlene and Leanne had little more furniture than their beds and personal objects like pictures and some kitchen equipment, so we went garage sale-ing in a big way. The one major piece of furniture I planned to get new was an adjustable armchair for Cath to sit in when she got uncomfortable in her wheelchair. I told Darlene I'd go hunting for one.

"You mean without Catherine?" she said indignantly.

"Well _"

"We're coming too. She should help choose it." So off we all set in the van (which Darlene already drove and which would be permanently at the girls' disposal once they moved in) while I once again ruminated on the pleasing realization that Darlene was a born advocate, even if it meant standing up to me.

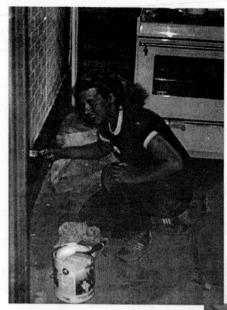

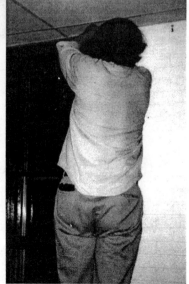

Zana paints, Ted fixes a rail - preparations

Moving Day - July. 18, 1986

The Path (completed) to 822 Preston
(Darlene's niece in the foreground)

Catherine moved into her new house on July 18th
1986. Darlene wheeled her through the kitchen and
into her bedroom. She didn't seem particularly
interested; she'd been there often before, so the
novelty had worn off. But when she saw her bed and
chest of drawers, which we'd already moved in,
something clicked and she did the most drawn-out
double take I've ever seen. Then she gave Darlene

and myself a bemused look and held up her left hand and stared at it for a long time, as if to check that it, at least, was still where it should be. Finally she smiled, just slightly. I found it difficult to leave and fussed around until finally Darlene pointed at the door.

"Home," she said. "You know we'll be fine."

"You've got my number?"

"Yes!" We hugged and I managed to leave without too many backward glances.

My friends had been informing me for months that I'd feel lost without Cath. Maybe that's why I didn't; I was almost over-prepared. She was, after all, only minutes away and for the time being, at least, I was still very much part of her life. Also, being able to sleep enough on a regular basis for the first time in a quarter of a century and being free to go out whenever I wanted to was, frankly, bliss. I sometimes stayed out late purely for the pleasure of knowing I didn't have to get up at 7.30 in the morning. Her leaving did have one curious effect, however. Coda our golden retriever and I continued to go for long rambles round the neighbourhood and it shook me to realize that without Cath I'd lost part of my identity. I was just a woman out for a walk with her dog.

The absence I really felt - cruelly - was that of the boys. They went to England "for a month, Mum" at about the same time that Cath moved out. Dominic ended up staying two years and Benjy, who has now become Ben, is still there over eleven years later.

If I didn't feel lost without Catherine for the first few days I certainly had trouble getting used to her absence. So did Ted. One evening he put down his current light reading, Isiah Berlin's **The Crooked Timber of Humanity**, and went into her room.

"I thought I heard her grinding her teeth," he said sheepishly when he got back.

"I keep hearing her mm-mm-mming," I said.

"She can always come back if it doesn't work."

"She cannot. This must and will work."

"Hm."

When I talk with other parents in various parts of the world I always stress that I was lucky to have had a husband who earned enough for us to live on, and that I appreciate having had the luxury of growing up with my children without having to get an outside job. Then I add that the other form of support he gave me was in the nature of an incentive: he invariably responded to my latest idea or plan about Cath with "It'll never work." The nods and smiles I get in response tell me that Ted isn't the only one.

He had refused steadfastly to go past, let alone enter Cath's house before she moved in and it was Darlene who finally lured him down there, well after everyone had settled in. None of us could reach high enough to put up curtain rails. "I'll get Ted," she announced (right from the start they had got on splendidly - much mutual respect) and twenty minutes later, somewhat to my chagrin, there he was, armed with a drill and a case of beer. Thenceforth, particularly while I was in England that August, he was a frequent and welcome visitor.

Celebration in the Park after moving into 822 Preston
Left to right: Marie, David, Sherrill, Leanne, Cath, Darlene,
Colleen, Evelyn & Lauchie

Letting Go is Hard

Catherine celebrates in the Jacuzzi with her friends -
as I head to England

Being in Sussex with the boys and my English
family and friends helped me start letting go of the
innate sense of responsibility I still felt about Cath,
even though she had officially left home and was, I
knew, secure and with wonderful room-mates. I
couldn't run down to her house and help if she had a
choke, I couldn't take down little plastic pots of her
favorite food, I couldn't sneak into her room at night
and make sure that Darlene and Leanne had
remembered to hitch her blankets into a tent over
her feet to prevent them being squashed down.

Nevertheless, I have to admit that I thought

about her frequently every day. When we were on the lawn having lunch - often great steaming heaps, all buttery, of scarlet runner beans from Mum's garden - I would visualize the girls, six hours behind us, rubbing their eyes and starting their day. I discovered later that, when I awoke at 8.00ish in the morning and fondly pictured Cath fast asleep and having lovely dreams she was often, instead, floating gloriously in the Jacuzzi with three or four friends while music played, incense burned and wine was imbibed - all at 2 a.m.

When I got back I was planning to go down to see Cath and the others as soon as I'd had a cup of tea with Ted and reported on the boys. But I was beaten to it. Cath looked round when she and Darlene came in and was plainly happy to be back in our house. She greeted us with unreserved pleasure. I noticed, though, that it was Darlene whom her eyes followed, not Ted or myself, and when Ted pushed her up the van ramp she craned her head around frantically to keep Darlene in sight.

A day or two later I went down to her house and, standing in front of her, rested my arms on her tray and beamed at her. Instead of the delighted beam back that I expected, my daughter, crossing her eyes with the effort, ground her teeth and gave me the most ferocious look in her repertoire and simultaneously swept me off her tray with her left arm. The she looked pointedly at the door and re-fused to let me catch her eye.

I was taken aback, but then realized she was communicating one of two important messages:

either she was saying this is *my* place so don't you dare move in, or else she was saying *this* is my place now so don't you dare take me back! Taking no chances that her meaning hadn't been made clear, she waited until about my fifth visitation before feeling relaxed enough to greet me with her usual welcoming smile.

Catherine, Dave, and Darlene

Circle of Friends

by Bob & Martha Perske
Abingdon Press (p.52)
(reprinted with permission)

Bob Perske & Circles of Friends

Bob Perske (top left) and friends at 822 Preston

During Darlene's two years with Cath, Bob Perske, an American journalist widely known both for his lifetime of work on behalf of people with disabilities and his books on the subject (beautifully illustrated by his wife Martha Perske), came to Winnipeg to collect stories for his book **Circles of Friends**. The book was to be subtitled People with Disabilities and Their Friends Enrich the Lives of One Another, and Bob reckoned Cath's lifestyle would be a fitting example of the subject. Rather than describe what Cath's household felt like from my point of view at the time, I'd like to quote parts of his article.

71

First, some comments from people living in the
house:

*"They pay us well at the hospital," said Lauchie,
"but I have this other satisfaction, coming home and
doing something for Catherine every now and then -
doing something that's freely given."*

*"We love it here," said Evelyn. "We are people who
are interested in good, basic living - we're not merely
interested in making money and getting ahead."
Little Marie showed her feelings by wanting to sit
next to Catherine when I took a picture of the group.*

*Colleen said she liked playing with money during
the day, but "I'm so much happier now that I'm
connected to the people in this house, too."*

*Leanne spoke of being away from her family for
the first time, and how good it felt to be part of this
family.*

Bob asked Darlene to comment on being
Catherine's friend and this was her response:

*"I was reluctant to talk," she said when asked
about her speech before the Canadian Association for
Community Living. "When I got up there I told them
I thought it was silly to even talk about it. It was just
so natural, being somebody's friend. But I talked
about Catherine and me going out with people and
being with people - about how she annoys me at times
- like when she grinds her teeth - and how I get on
her nerves and we straighten things out. She really
is my friend. She knows more about me than any-
body else. (laughs) Gee! If Catherine ever speaks, the
stories she could tell (more laughter). She knows*

everything that goes on, she just has her own way of communicating, and I don't see that as her disability - it's mine. I have to learn her language....For the last few months I've been going through a lot of different things in my life. And Cath rubs my face or takes my hand and squeezes it ...she gives, too."

Darlene then talked about entertainment, and on support from other members of the house.

"We go everywhere; lots of friends drop by to go out with her, too. We go dancing where people aren't worried about the wheelchair. Leanne went with her to a school play. We saw the film *Crocodile Dundee* which she loved - and *Witches of Eastwick* - which I loved and she hated. We even go out to four-course dinners."

"Don't forget about the male strippers," Leanne added. She and Darlene looked at Nicola and laughed.

Nicola laughed, too. "I'd never have gone with her," she said, "but three of her friends did a couple of years ago, and Cath thought it was wonderful. Giggled all the way through, and nonstop for several days afterward."

"It's really neat," Darlene said, "we never lock our doors. If I have to leave for awhile, I can open my door and let the rest know, and I know everything will be okay. Also, because there's always somebody in the house, no crook would ever try to get away with something."

Bob Perske then commented: "During the day I spent at their house, every renter made me welcome. I

73

watched Darlene's concern for Leanne, who was
coming down with a cold. I saw her work confidently
with Catherine, who suddenly choked on a cracker.
She joined with others to borrow some of Lauchie's
tools to get a flat tire off Catherine's wheelchair and
hustled to various shops until she found one that
would fit. Then she fixed a meal for Catherine,
Leanne, Colleen, and me.

   At dinner, Catherine, who swiped a glance at me
every now and then but still refused to make eye
contact, let me know her jury was still out on whether
to accept me.

   At the end of the evening everyone in the house
gathered and talked about their life together (for my
benefit). They saw great humor in a government
licensing man who came with his clipboard to see if
Catherine was being cared for properly. Seemingly
unable to sense the richness of the personal interactions
in the house, he wrote them up for a lack of draperies
in the kitchen.

   As people began to sum up their experience,
Joanne (a friend) touched on something they all
seemed to feel: "Catherine laughs at me a lot. She
makes me feel warm." Laughter is her litmus test for
accepting one as a friend.'

I can't, of course, resist adding to what Bob wrote.
For instance, whenever I dropped by the house in
those two years there was always at least one, often
more like four or five, of Darlene's and Leanne's
friends there and Cath was always part of whatever
was going on. I had lunch today with two women

whom I've known for years because we all have daughters who have disabilities. Their daughters are teenagers now and planning is afoot for their moving away from home.

Remembering the profound effect Darlene had on Cath's life I told my friends that, in looking for people to live with their daughters it will be essential for those people, as well as having a good set of personal values, to be outgoing and to have a wide circle of friends themselves, and to be well-connected to the community at large. When Catherine left home she didn't, if I'm honest, have any of her own friends, as distinct from people who were also, and usually primarily, my friends. Now, through Darlene and the other people who have lived with her in the last few years, she truly does.

There are many stories that could be told that demonstrate the distinctive and cheerful - albeit sometimes pandemonious - nature of the household.

For instance, the owner of the nearby corner store, Kedar, had saved enough money to buy a house in the neighbourhood and his wife was coming from India to join him. However, they needed somewhere to live for a month before their house became vacant. They were delighted when Darlene, Leanne and Cath invited them to camp out in the basement, with shared use of the kitchen, and it became a mutually satisfying experience (delectable curries, for one thing). I loved the idea that Catherine, originally predicted by doctors never to be anything but a burden, was now giving refuge to some people in trouble.

A cameo: Marie was overheard introducing two of her nursery school friends to Catherine. "This is my friend Catherine," she said. After a pause she added, "and she lives with two handicapped women." Apparently she knew the word came into the picture somewhere but wasn't sure to whom it applied!

Marie and Catherine

Another cameo: That Darlene and Leanne were living with Cath as friends, rather than just as helpers, was epitomized one day in a brief exchange:

Me: Hey Leanne, that's Cath's sweater you're wearing.

Leanne: Sure - I really like it!

Me: Oh, I see.

Leanne: And Cath's wearing Darlene's harem pants - they look great on her, don't they? And Darlene's borrowed those crystal earrings Cath got for her birthday. We all wear each others' clothes...

One more cameo: Darlene had a bad shoulder and Lauchie and Evelyn had been lifting Cath several times a day on a regular basis. I was thanking Evelyn for this long-term, cheerfully given assistance.

"You really don't have to thank us, Nicola," she said, "Cath's the reason we're living here." Then she added a comment that made me tingle. "Cath," she said, "is the heart of our household."

Mention of Joanne in Bob's article reminds me that she and her friend Brad spent many a day with Cath. As well as being able to offer Darlene free room and board and a small (embarrassingly small) stipend, l'Avenir could afford, through Government "respite" funding, to give her about thirty hours of time off a week. She chose to take this in the form of a forty-eight hour weekend every two weeks and one evening a week. She was encouraged to find people from among her friends to take over with Cath and this she had no trouble doing.

Like Darlene, Joanne and Brad were students and moving in with Cath periodically suited them well. Darlene, meanwhile, if she didn't spend the weekend with her family, crashed with Ted and myself, which was a pleasure for us. Several other couples and individuals spent time with Cath and while each person brought different and interesting qualities to Cath's life, they all had one thing in common: a fondness for Cath and, as part of that fondness, an appreciation of what they could learn from her. "I'd never met someone who was unable to walk or talk," said one and them, giving voice to what many people have indicated over the years. "Cath taught me to value my abilities. She made me think."

When Leanne left after a year to work in Peru, I asked a mutual friend of Cath's, Darlene's and mine if he would consider moving in. His name was David, but to distinguish him from the David who had already had such an impact of Cath's life I'll call him Dave. Quiet and thoughtful, Dave was in his mid-twenties and headed for a career in business administration. However, just prior to our meeting him he had taken a job sorting out the finances of a forty bed group home. He was so horrified by the conditions in which people were living that he started a community agency, similar in ways to l'Avenir, to help them find better housing and daytime activities. When I first asked him if he would be interested in living with Cath, his main concern was whether, with the demands of running the agency, he would have the time and energy he'd like to give Cath as a roommate.

The agreement in the house, via Prairie Housing Coop, was that all members of the household should meet and approve a new person moving in.

Everyone liked Dave and he made the decision to move in. He ended up staying for two and a half years. He made it clear from the start that he was Catherine's friend, which precluded his doing anything she disliked, such as coercing her to drink when she was ill. Cath appeared to appreciate this and I recall many a time seeing her reach out and touch Dave with love and gratitude illuminating her face.

Dave also proved to be a thoughtful advocate for Cath. When the van developed so many holes in the floor that she was in danger of sinking through it, we started discussing a new one. Dave suggested designing the adaptations so that Cath sat in the front next to the driver, rather than being stuck behind the driver and having a nonstop view of his or her hair and shoulders. This was a novel idea and I don't think it would have occurred to me. It was tricky to accomplish but we did it, and Cath for several years now has shared a front seat view - and coffee - with whoever is driving.

Dave is now a family man and a lawyer (in which capacity he has, among other cases, represented several people with disabilities who are in conflict with the law) so the amount of time he spends with Cath these days has inevitably diminished significantly - part of the ebb and flow of any friendship. I'm so convinced of his fundamental fidelity to her, however, that he is one of the trustees of the fund set up in her name in my Will.

I asked Dave to write about his time with Cath.

One of the first times I met Catherine was when I went to her house for a small gathering - probably intended to evaluate my worthiness as a potential roommate to Cath. After I had answered and asked questions a number of us, including Catherine, got into the whirlpool. Sitting in the Jacuzzi with Catherine's head on my chest I knew that we would get along well. I remember feeling very peaceful and happy. Catherine's smiles and chuckles and her gentle kicking lifted my spirits.

Catherine has the gift of the subtle. No one else I know can brighten my mood with a smile or a chuckle like Catherine can. When she smiles at me or touches my hand I feel loved - no small gift.

Not only does Catherine give gently, she accepts tenderness and gentleness. She allowed me to be gentle - to speak softly, sit quietly, stroke her hand or let her stroke mine - without any discomfort. I don't feel self-conscious when I'm with Catherine.

I lived with Catherine during a period of inner struggle, and she made me calm. I felt that I could share what I was feeling with her without a lot of words. Being together in contented silence is one of the important mutual gifts of friendship.

As I write, I realize that Catherine provided an anchor for me. She gave me a home that I loved, she is a completely non-judgmental friend, she made me feel loved, and helped me define myself. I am extremely grateful to her for her friendship.

Darlene had made a two year commitment to live with Cath. After that she was due to practice teaching for a year and knew she would be too preoccupied to be Cath's primary caregiver. As the end of her reign approached I started, reluctantly, to put out feelers for a replacement. Fittingly, it was Catherine herself who found new people to live with her.

New People

Laurie, Elke and Cath

L'Avenir had grown considerably in the interim and under Cindy's auspices had moved away from ACL Winnipeg to become a separate entity. Prairie Housing had also become much larger and now included a large downtown apartment block with twenty-seven units, the acquisition and setting-up of which had been engineered by David. This co-op, too, had moved away from ACL. I suspect David felt somewhat miffed and somewhat concerned when these two gangling teenagers struck out on their own but, like any good father, he has since then always been on hand to give support and assistance.

When Cindy left due to her husband being transferred to the North West Territories, her place as General Manager was taken by our enthusiastic and upbeat friend Sandee, who had previously been connected with the Red River Community College project. Sandee had obtained the services of a warm and empathic young woman called Laurie to act as l'Avenir's 'individual support worker.' This position involved working closely with Sandee and, particularly, spending time with l'Avenir's members and ensuring that their needs and wishes were being heard and, if possible, met.

It was in this capacity that Laurie had gotten to know Cath and she and her husband Glen decided that, if everyone approved, they'd like to live with Cath. Cath seemed to think it a good idea, especially when Glen serenaded her with his guitar. Dave was agreeable, so in they moved with their two cats. Realizing that Laurie would find it burdensome to be l'Avenir's support worker full-time now that she had responsibilities to Cath, she and Glen, who had experience working in the respite and teacher's aide field, decided to job share both as Cath's roommates and at l'Avenir.

At this time Lauchie and Evelyn concluded that they needed to return to the l'Arche community (they're still there, and we're all still friends). An amiable married couple, Eileen and Gerald, whom I'd met through talking to a University of Manitoba nurses' class, moved in upstairs. I was glad, and doubtless Cath was too, that Dave and Colleen stayed put and provided not only assistance but continuity.

Inevitably, the tenor of the house changed, particularly in Catherine's apartment. Cath may have missed the buzz that Darlene and her friends provided but seemed content with the quieter atmosphere provided by Laurie and Glen. They were both creative people and the basement became a double studio, half for Laurie and her pottery and half for Glen and his music. Much of their creativity took place in the kitchen and sittingroom, though, and Cath loved it when Glen played his guitar and sang and when the cats got tied up in the piles of wool that Laurie was weaving into a wall hanging.

Tensions

For a few months all went well. Then a number of factors combined to create tension. Chief among these were Catherine's health, or lack thereof, and unexpected and traumatic personal problems between Glen and Laurie which, they have been consistently anxious to assure me, had nothing to do with Catherine. Glen left the house after a year but Laurie stayed another few months until the spring of 1990. Since I knew about what was happening but was essentially on the periphery, I'd like to quote what Glen wrote when I asked him recently to contribute to Cath's story:

The year that I spent living with Cath was a difficult one personally, but not without its pleasures. I miss the feeling of community and mutual concern

*that the circle of people around Cath shared. We
also had some great, fun times together. I do wonder
sometimes if I ever saw Cath at her best. She had
such a hard winter physically that year. During
those bouts of illness, just getting enough fluids
into her became a battle, with her stubbornness
more than a match for us. That year Catherine
was certainly witness to enough emotional upheaval
to last a lifetime. Late at night after we had gone
to bed, Laurie and I would often hear Cath happily
giving the bunch of us a big raspberry. With a
whirlwind blowing around her, I thought she was
more than entitled.*

When I asked Laurie about her time with Cath
she chose to write Cath a letter. Parts of it follow:

*It was not an easy time for either of us, was it,
Cath? You were sick so much of the time...and the
struggle we had to figure out what was wrong with
you. Most of the answers came later, after I'd left.*

*I remember days of knowing you were feeling
lousy or hurting, and I'd be desperately searching
for every available clue to solve the riddle of what
was ailing you. I hated the fact you were in pain
and I didn't know how to relieve it. Do you
remember the times when all else failed and I'd
settle you on your bed, light up the candles, put
Vivaldi on the tape deck and give you a full body
massage? Both you and I knew that wasn't getting
to the root of the problem but you were gracious in
your appreciation and took from it what comfort
you could. Do you remember all the horrible treat-*

ments and remedies we put you through, Cath? If
you're like me you've probably blocked as much of
it from your mind as you could. Let's see now...for
chest infections there was the treatment consisting
of alternating hot and cold packs on your back and
cold wet cotton socks covered with warm woolly
ones...for urinary tract infections there was that
extremely effective but thoroughly obnoxious-tasting
concoction referred to as your pee-pipe tea...and if
you started twisting around in your wheelchair
and grabbing at us (a sure sign your back was out
of whack) it would be time for your favourite treatment of all - Tracey the Chiropractor! As bizarre
as some of it sounds, it really did help.

Intermixed with all the struggles were some
very good times as well; for example, those quiet
cozy evenings with your dad, being plied with
liqueur and chocolates while discussing philosophy.
We also benefited from the experience of living in a
communal house with the various exchanges and
gatherings that that entailed.

My time with you as your roommate was one of
the most challenging of my life. It facilitated some
of my greatest growth. It was also the birthplace
of myself as an independent being.

So thank you, Cath, for sharing yourself and
your home with me. Most of all, thanks for hanging
in there through all the good times and the bad.

The way Catherine's mind works, her thought
processes, remain a mystery. I'm certain, however,
that she has thirty-six years' worth of questions to

ask and comments to make. I'm equally certain that the worst aspect of her disability, for her, is that when she's in pain she can't get across where the pain is, its degree and what relieves it. For those around her who want desperately to help her when she's hurting it's gut-wrenchingly frustrating not to know these details.

Sometimes it's pretty obvious what's wrong. If, for instance, she has a fever and cough and doesn't want to swallow it's a safe bet she has an upper respiratory infection, including a sore throat. Often, though, as with most people, there's no discernible reason for the pain, even when, carefully watching her expression, we manipulate various limbs and joints or press different areas of her abdomen.

Occasionally she really confuses us, too, when we think she should be in agony but isn't, like the times when I've caught her foot wheeling around a doorway - something that, if done to me would cause an outburst of yelling and swearing but to which she reacts with every sign of riotous enjoyment.

She has had some horrible health problems in the last few years. Even towards the end of Darlene's time with her she began to indicate, by biting her hand and by her expression, that she was sometimes in significant pain. Analgesics didn't seem to help and none of us liked the symptomatic approach anyway. She was also getting food stuck in her esophagus more frequently and this often led to pneumonia because she aspirated the mucus that collected above the jammed food. Her esophagus was, we discovered, becoming scarred by acid rolling back up it and she was taking huge amounts of antacid glop. As Laurie indicated in her letter, Cath also started getting urinary tract or, as we referred to them, pee-pipe infections. This is one of the many problems common to people who spend much of their time sitting in a wheelchair.

We soon learned to recognize the symptoms and got her onto antibiotics. The trouble was that at times she seemed to be on the damned stuff for weeks at time and then have to start again shortly afterwards when the infection flared up once more.

When Laurie and Glen moved in with Cath the above problems became quite worrying, and involved pain for Cath and concern on Laurie's and Glen's part. Laurie helped in two important ways. My method of dealing with a jammed esophagus, which I had taught Darlene by demonstration, was first to panic, then to control the panic and then to try to induce vomiting (on Cath's part). While this often worked it was a traumatizing procedure for all concerned and, when it didn't work, meant yet another trip to the hospital. Laurie called me one night to say that Cath had had a choke but that whatever had been stuck had apparently made its way down into her stomach.

"Well done," I said. "Okay, how? You sound pleased with yourself."

"Candles and soft music and stroking," she said, and beamed.

"The calm approach. Not a bad idea." And sure enough, her method both worked more often than not and was far less intrusive.

Laurie also introduced Cath and myself to an extraordinary naturopath, Dr. Goodheart. One of the many ways he helped Cath was to prescribe and procure the special tea for her pee-pipe infections. It's a magical mixture of herbs and berries and smells delicious when it's being brewed, although I agree with Laurie that it tastes vile unless camouflaged. It also does the trick, on a consistent basis; in the eight years that Cath has been using this tea she's only once, due to extenuating circumstances, had to resort to chemical antibiotics.

Laurie and Glen and I between us may have given the impression that during this time Catherine was constantly ill or in pain. This was not so. Much of the time she appeared healthy and happy and thoroughly enjoyed life; it was just that when she did have problems she was so utterly wretched. Also, we always felt, even when she had recovered from a serious infection, that she had an underlying fundamental problem that we hadn't identified.

Adventures In Riding Mountain

Sonja and Cath at Riding Mountain Park

Cath has the ability to attract unusual people. The first time I met Sonja she was sporting leather anklets with little bells attached, so when I say she was unusual with bells on I mean it literally as well as figuratively. She came into Cath's life to lend support to Laurie when Glen left and, to a greater or lesser extent, has remained linked to her since that time.

Her main responsibility was to ensure that Cath had fun at weekends and my friends often reported seeing Cath and 'a lovely young woman with long hair, round glasses and a huge smile' at, for example, a farmers' market out in the country or participating

in Winnipeg's annual March for Peace. Sonja had
the use of a house in the middle of nowhere near
Riding Mountain National Park and, accompanied by
friends, took Cath up there for several holidays. It
couldn't have been easy - no running water for one
thing - but Sonja made it work and Cath has photos
of herself and friends lying on the grass under a tree
and being wheeled down the beach with Sonja's dogs
bounding along at her side.

Sonja has written:

*I had grown up scared of people with disabilities
and generally avoided them, so I was apprehensive
when I went to meet Cath. (A friend had told me
Cath was looking someone to spend time with her.)
During that first meeting in her living room I
remember the way she observed me without a
smile - but curious all the time. When I looked at
her she looked away; when I looked away she
looked at me. It was like playing hide and seek. I
can't remember what broke through my first layer
of concerns. Maybe it was Cath's softness that I
sensed even that first time I saw her. Maybe it was
the confidence I got from her wonderful
housemates.*

*When I started work two weeks later my heart
was pounding and my hands shaking. I didn't
want to do the wrong thing or hurt Cath by mistake.
It took me a while to learn all her disabilities but
during that same time I learned about her abilities
- her charm, her softness, her humour.*

*It wasn't always easy to be there for Cath. The
emotional demand was often more than one person*

could carry. After all, you're constantly trying to talk for someone else, understand her feelings, her desires, her needs. She made me realize that when I was with her I, too, was disabled. At first I made decisions for her - like where to spend our evenings and with whom, without even telling her beforehand where we were going. I apologized to her for this and told her I hoped she didn't mind me taking the freedom to make decisions.

There were many people that I met through Cath, and she shared some of my friends with me. As a rather new resident of the city (I had come from Germany two years previously) I was glad to have Cath as a friend through whom I could without much effort make new friends. Whenever I spent time with her I realized that somehow everybody took to her no matter where we went. Often I would walk down the street - more or less stumbling behind that wheelchair - and someone would walk up to us - or better, Cath - and say 'Hi, I'm so-and-so, I saw you coming down the street...I'm a good friend of Cath's, I've known her since she was... Cath, it's so good to see you. How are you doing?' It always surprised me how many people knew Cath. It was almost like she was a celebrity.

Many people I've met through Cath have become close friends of mine. These are people like Tandy and Gavin, who once lived in Cath's house and who taught me so much about the 'new age' lifestyle during the 'Year of Aquarius.' We spent many hours in the house philosophizing with these groovy people. Then there was Dave, who would not miss breakfast with us - and we laughed because Cath always reached for his coffee, preferring it to her own. And Laurie, who taught us that drinking lots of water will give us the clean-looking face that we envied her for.

Cath has a charm that attracts people the first time they meet her, and she doesn't even have to smile. During a wondrous week in Riding Mountain among colourful birds, busy bees and the company of friends, we were invited to a big feast and afterwards we roasted marshmallows over the bonfire. I was so taken aback by this new Canadian discovery that I didn't notice right away that Cath had disappeared. I ran around asking everyone where she was and then I saw her coming down the lane with two of my friends. 'We just went for a walk...'

I think that working, spending time with Cath helped me reflect on how I perceive people and what kind of value I put on their abilities or disabilities. My time with her has taken away my fear of disabled people in general and has led me to an understanding of the joys, frustrations and fears of an individual friend.

Cath and Sonja obviously had some great times together and Sonja's positive attitude must, by osmosis, have given Cath a psychological boost.

One of my favourite stories about Sonja and Cath, which Sonja told me with great amusement, was the time they went to a party and a guy came smiling up to their table. Sonja didn't feel like dancing and was preparing to decline politely, but when the guy reached their table he asked Cath to dance.

And then, in the fall of 1990, came Rika. Sonja wasn't able to live with Catherine full-time and no-one else materialized. So, for the first time since Cath moved into her own home we had to advertise in the paper for live-in assistants. It made me nervous.

At the beginning of 1989 a huge party was held by members, relatives, staff and friends of l'Avenir to bid farewell to Sandee, who had put in several years of sterling work as General Manager. We were most reluctant to see her leave but had to agree that she had a valid reason: she and her husband were expecting their first baby. Fortunately we had to look no further than our own Board to find a new General Manager.

Cheryl was a close friend of one of our members and had been on the Board for two years, so she already had a good idea of how the organization worked. She also knew what a complex and some-times frightening job it was to make it work well. Rare were the days when Sandee had been able to sit in the office *merely* answering the phone, filling out Government forms, writing letters, interviewing potential staff, dealing with current staff problems, meeting with members or their families or, with Gloria our invaluable bookkeeper, sorting out our convoluted finances. However, Cheryl did take over and was well entrenched by the time Rika appeared. She responded to the newspaper ad and Cheryl was plainly impressed by her. "She's a bit young," said Cheryl when, after interviewing her, she invited me to meet Rika, "but I think she'll suit Cath."

I walked into Cath's sittingroom where she, looking down at her left hand thoughtfully, had gathered with a number of others. Gavin and Tandy, a friendly and very helpful pair who lived upstairs, were there, as was Rod, a friend of Cath's and mine of many years standing who now inhabited the bachelor apartment and whose regular assistance to Cath included helping her out of bed each morning (she loved that)before he went to work. Lloyd, too, was present; he was a philosopher/carpenter who shared Cath's apartment for awhile and contributed deep thoughts and trails of wood shavings. The only person I didn't know was a striking woman with short black hair, black clothes and a ring in her nose. She looked about twenty and was quiet and wary.

Cheryl had fudged a little. Rika was in fact only just eighteen but, as I was soon to discover, was one of the most responsible and resourceful people ever to enhance my daughter's life. She took Cath's health problems in her considerable stride and learned quickly that the best way of dealing with me was to highlight the positive and downplay problems - rather in the same way that I dealt with Ted, come to think of it.

She did once give me a hell of a fright by phoning me in England. When Ben said it was Rika on the phone I could barely say hello but she sensibly prefaced what she had to say with, "Cath's fine, just fine." By that time Rika had organized a women's drumming circle and Cath was a fully qualified member, contributing beats on her drum when the spirit moved her. Rika wanted to know if I was prepared to pay for a magnificent but expensive rain stick (an unusual and easy-to-play percussive instrument) she'd found and which she thought Cath would like. I said yes, of course. What she didn't tell me, till I got back, was that Cath had just recovered from pneumonia.

Rika was - is - a human rights activist and, like Sonja, an assertive feminist. She had a circle of similarly-minded friends, mainly women, who all seemed to wear black, to change their hair colour frequently, to wear exotic jewelry and to clump around either in army boots or black Doc Martens. They took Cath under their collective wing, always including her in whatever was going on and giving her lots of attention.

My friends were constantly informing me that they'd seen Cath at the Legislature at a Take Back The Night demonstration or on TV at a neighbourhood rally of some sort. There were sightings all over town, and further afield. In the summer of 1993, Rika, her friend Christine and Cath took off in the van for ten days to a ten thousand-strong women's music camp in Michigan and they met several Winnipeg friends of mine there. I myself had a curious experience during Rika's reign. My dog and I were ambling down a local street which had been blocked off to traffic for a street festival. Amidst the cheerful crowds I saw a woman approaching in a wheelchair. She was wearing sun glasses, an elegant velvet hat and a flowing flowery dress. She was accompanied by three women, one of whom had orange hair and who waved when she saw me. It was Rika. I had recognized neither her nor my daughter.

Members of Rika's entourage frequently moved in and out of Cath's house, sometimes because they needed somewhere to stay and other times because Rika needed help with Cath. They also often came to visit me singly or en masse with Cath - and I found their company both stimulating and entertaining. It made me realize that, with the boys gone, Cath and her friends have consistently helped me keep up with what my mother used to call 'the young.' I appreciate that.

Cath at the Women's Music Camp in Michigan - 1993

Medical Crises

On most occasions when Catherine has needed help at the Health Sciences Centre she and the friends (or me) who have taken her there have been pleased with the treatment, both medical and psychological, that we've received. On a fateful day in the summer of 1990, however, this was not the case. The person staying with Cath at the time called me to say that Cath had part of her supper, a chick pea, stuck in her esophagus and that the calm approach hadn't worked so she'd called an ambulance. I met them at the hospital and we spent literally hours suctioning Cath while waiting for action. Usually a surgeon would have checked her and had her down to an operating room quite quickly but this time, despite continually being told that a surgeon would appear imminently, none did.

By midnight Cath's friend was exhausted so I suggested she go home. About an hour later I realized that Cath was in real trouble. By now too tired to cough up the constantly gathering mucus, she simply quit and the next thing I knew she was going blue around the edges and her eyes were rolling up and she went limp. I shouted to a nurse and finally there was action. An on-stretcher X-ray was taken, after which she was rushed into the resuscitation room where a medley of medics crowded around her. I was told categorically to keep out ("the doctors are busy.") In sudden and desperate need of moral support I phoned Darlene, who appeared within minutes. We huddled together miserably.

Ted is an inveterate but silent worrier and we came to an arrangement years ago where I tell him afterwards, when things are fine again, that Cath has been in trouble. This time, however, I phoned him too, since I'd been given no assurance by the doctors that Cath would survive. We'll do our best, they'd said. I told Ted that Darlene was coming down and that I'd call when I knew more. He was all prepared to come down but as it happened one of the doctors swung out of the resuscitation room and told us Cath was breathing properly again. We sped to her side and she glared at us crossly and then looked away.

I was too shaken to ask questions. I did discover, however, that the bloody chick pea was still stuck and that there was still nobody around who could remove it. I don't know about anyone else, but I know how horrible it is to swallow something too large and it gets stuck even for an instant on its way down. The idea of having an object jammed for hours at a time is appalling. Cath was first on the operating list that morning but that was still two or three hours away. The rest of the night is a blank but I imagine I continued to suction her when necessary - about every ten minutes - until she was prepared for surgery.

Cath and I hadn't met the surgeon, T.H., before but he was friendly. He came to talk to me afterwards and told me that the crisis a few hours earlier had been due to her left lung having collapsed due, in turn, to being clogged up with mucus. He also said that her esophagus was a mess as a result not only of the chick pea having been stuck there for about twelve hours but also to scarring from previous blockages. He wanted to do another esophagoscopy in a couple of months.

By that time Rika was living with Cath and I went down with the two of them for what we assumed was a checkup. We met Dr. T.H. while Cath was recovering from the anesthetic.

"The good news is that there's no additional scarring. But," Dr. T.H. paused, "we took some X-rays and Catherine has a hiatus hernia, which we'll have to repair, and a large growth of some sort either in her uterus or on an ovary which will also have to be dealt with. The pain she's been having is a result of excessive acid re-entering her esophagus." He showed us the X-ray and explained that the purpose of the diaphragm muscle is to keep the lungs and esophagus up and the stomach and guts down. In Cath's case there was a hole, so part of her stomach was knocking around in her chest and squashing her esophagus. Very nasty.

While the news was horrifying, it did explain the distress she'd been experiencing for so long, which was obviously far worse than mere heartburn. We took Catherine to a gynecologist and an ultrasound showed that the cyst, or whatever it was, spread right across her lower abdomen. I had for some time thought I could feel something in that area which, after feeling my own body, seemed strange but it had been explained away whenever I'd asked a doctor about it.

The two doctors involved agreed to get together, each to do his and her part of the operation, and a date was set. In the meantime we conferred with a dietitian at the hospital who gave us a diet for Cath that excluded fat and acid. Thenceforth, too, Cath had to eat two sorts of pill at frequent intervals; one to reduce the amount of acid her stomach normally produced and the other to speed up the digestive process. The eating aspect of her life, always one she had particularly enjoyed, must have seemed boring at that time but these measures did reduce the pain significantly.

We awaited the operation date impatiently and were more than a little irritated when it had to be delayed due to a nurses' strike (which I agreed with in principle). Dr. T.H. promised that Cath would be at the top of the list once the strike ended and the operation eventually took place on February 25th, 1990.

Then I Wrote a Letter

Since reluctantly giving up playing the cello many years ago, I've subsequently enjoyed music-making vicariously by being on the Board of the Manitoba Chamber Orchestra and acting as what might loosely be called production manager. This can mean anything from ensuring that the stage goes up and down, the musicians on and off it and the guest artists in and out (of the airport) at the right times. It also includes hanging around at rehearsals, purportedly to run errands if necessary for Simon

Streatfeild, our esteemed music director and conductor, or other musicians but really because I just love to be there.

I was grateful that while Cath was in surgery the orchestra was rehearsing for a concert. Rennie, until recently our principal violist, and Simon both gave me encouraging hugs when I told them what was going on. Sitting in Westminster United Church, where our concerts are held, and listening to Gorecki's Three Pieces in the Olden Style and Robert Turner's Manitoba Memoir were a far better distraction than the hospital cafeteria.

I had been warned that it would take up to eight months for Catherine to recover fully from her double surgery but I'd thought this was an exaggeration. Not so. While she did slowly gain strength and was certainly cheerful much of the time, the operation and the period leading up to it must have seriously weakened her body and made her less resistant than usual to infections. I can probably best describe the months after the operation by quoting the following letter.

I wrote it between 1.30 and 3.30 p.m. on October 20th 1991 at the end of a women's poetry-writing weekend that I had the pleasure of accommodating in my house. Although I wasn't part of the workshop (I just sort of lurked, made coffee, chatted with people during breaks, etc.), I was encouraged by Di Brandt - the Winnipeg poet leading the event - and the other inspiring women present to produce a poem. I can't cope with poetry but realized I did have something churning around inside me that had to emerge in

101

one form or another. Hence the letter. It's virtually unchanged since I wrote it, the significance of which is that, as a ponderous writer I would normally have struggled with such an outpouring for days and then fiddled with it endlessly. But I wanted to be like everyone else and write within the given time limit. So it's rough and raw but, by golly, it's real. I was deeply grateful to Di and company for affording me the unexpected opportunity to sort out the disturbing thoughts and emotions I'd been experiencing:

Cath, my darling girl:

It's been a grim two years for you in many ways, hasn't it? Months of acid burning its way up your esophagus, months of intermittent pneumonia and gurgly coughing, months of pee-pipe infections, months of feeling exhausted, months of doctors and technicians handling - sometimes far from gently - your battered body, months of those (to you at least) needless needles, months of having unwanted food and fluids forced into you, months of blocked bowels and the consequent assaults on your system, months of your mother's face looming gloomily over you as, once again, you were in discernible but indecipherable pain. And perhaps - though none of us can do more than guess what goes on in that mysterious mind of yours - perhaps months of wondering when the people around you would figure out what was wrong and the pain and indignities would end.

Well, we finally did sort out some of the problems, and that resulted in your waking up one day with a row of clips and stitches and pain from your sternum to your crotch. They had repaired your hiatus hernia ("huge," said the thoracic surgeon, "I could put my fist through it,") and removed a (benign) cyst from one of your ovaries."It was like eight oranges strung together," said the gynecologist.

That was in February '91, and we all looked forward to your gradual recovery, thankful to think that your troubles were over. But it seemed that as soon as we started rejoicing with you as you began once again to enjoy eating, to enjoy going for walks, to enjoy being in the pool, to enjoy going to the bar with friends, to enjoy life, things started to go wrong again. I reached a point where the phone ringing caused my stomach to seize up, where I had to take several deep breaths to listen to the messages on my bloody answering machine, where it took all my courage merely to call your house or drop in to see how you were. And as, time and again, I rushed down - after an alarmed and alarming call from one of your splendid and empathic room-mates and helpers - and found you feverish, whimpering, gagging, defenseless, totally wretched, I began to have black thoughts about what your life felt like to you. Were you willing to go through all this pain and discomfort, then to be made better, only to face more pain and discomfort soon afterwards?

Until recently you'd had a pretty good life. Maybe you were saying hey, let's leave it at that, my body seems to be falling apart, let me go.

I found these thoughts terrifying and unmentionable.
In the past, my love, I've only worried and
grieved when you've actually been ill, and the rest
of the time have been joyful about your life. But
now I find I worry and grieve not only when you're
in trouble but all the time. And I extend that worry
and grief into the future. I've almost stopped
daring to hope that you'll be well more often than
ill. I'm becoming a half-empty rather than a half-full
person as far as you're concerned. I find it safer; I
expect trouble and can be grudgingly happy when
it's absent.

Last week, when you'd been staying with me
because I could no longer stand the strain of waiting
for the inevitable, it seemed to me, emergency
phone call, you seemed to be getting well and
happy but suddenly developed a raging fever and
shrank with dehydration within a couple of hours.
Rika and I took you to the hospital and two doctors
said you were fighting for your life. As, trembling,
I invaded your armpits with cold wet cloths and a
nurse invaded your bottom with Tylenol
suppositories - all to reduce your fever - I began
again to wonder. Do you want us to do this? Is that
sunken-eyed look you're giving me one of anger and
despair at not being heard? Have you had enough?

I'm sure my hot tears streaming onto your burning
body could hardly have helped you but at least
some of the horrors I was and had been having for
months were being released.

My black thoughts did not evaporate with my
tears and will probably return but you did something

for me last night, a week after your recovery from that particular trauma and your return to your home, that greatly ameliorated my misery. I visited you, after managing to be out of touch for nearly forty-eight hours, and was ready to find you experiencing some new wretchedness. Your friend Rika greeted me. "Nicola! Stop looking so worried, Cath's had a great day, she's been so happy! It's been wonderful, we've been laughing together all day!" And there you were, all pink and healthy and you greeted me with a huge smile and that chirrup of excitement and shake of your body that tells me you're feeling really good.

And that made me remember something of the utmost importance about you, a quality that many, including myself, could and should learn from you: as soon as you've recovered from something nasty you seem able to dismiss it, and are ready to enjoy life again. I know you don't forget it. But you don't dwell on it and worry about it happening again - until it happens.

I think you truly take life not only a day at a time but a moment at a time. Brilliant! I intend to do the same. I am a half-full person, even where you're concerned, and you've reminded me of that. Thank you, my precious girl.

From then on, almost exactly eight months since the operation, Cath's health improved greatly.

Transitions

I was seriously upset when Rika, after living with
Cath for a year and a half, out of the blue told me
she was quitting as Cath's roommate.

"But Rika you've seen her through all the ghastly
stuff - her operations and the aftermath - and things
really have improved now, I mean Cath's health has,
and surely it's easier now and more fun and anyway
I thought you liked being with Cath!"

"Calm down, Nicola, I'm not just walking out. I'll
be around to help someone else move in. I love Cath,
but I need to move on. Anyway," she added as I
yanked another Kleenex out of the box, "I want to
stay on as her weekend person. It's time she and I
just had some fun." That helped, and I was even
able, after calling her a cheeky cow, to agree to being
used as a reference for the job she was after.

I whined about Rika's imminent departure to
several friends, including Di Brandt the next time
she gave a women's writing workshop in my house.
We were once again looking for two people, preferably
a settled couple, and although Di didn't know such a
combination, she did suggest that her sister-in-law
Irene, who had recently moved to Winnipeg, might
be interested. She recommended her highly, so
meetings and interviews were duly set up and Irene,
who was willing to take on the challenge, moved in.

At first blush, Irene appeared quiet and reserved
but like so many young women from a Mennonite
background, including Darlene and Di, she proved to
have an intense inner life that was busting its way

out. In Irene's case it was through art, and her distinctive and accomplished work enlivened Cath's apartment during the time she was there. Cath, typically, took her time sizing up Irene, but I pointed out to both of them that the period of comparative tranquillity and orderliness that I suspected Irene could provide might be just what Cath needed after the busy fall. Irene remained relatively retiring with me but her letter describing her time with Cath reveals what went on between the two of them:

The seven and a half months that I spent as Cath's helper and roommate were filled with learning, laughter and occasional tears as two headstrong, independent-thinking women met head to head, both believing their way was best. Originally I often looked upon this time as an opportunity to help Cath gain more independence; often, however, she became the teacher and I learned things about myself, relationships, and life.

Cath, a young woman who sits unspeaking in a wheelchair watching life go by? Never! She often gets more enjoyment from life than people who are able-bodied. Good-natured, loving, laughing, Cath frequently communicates more in her own way than words do. Caring, giving, she enjoys walks on a summer evening, music, theatre and parties. She has a special gift of acceptance and I often found myself singing, playing and talking with Cath as I didn't do with friends I'd known for years.

I knew that Irene would find it tough going living with Cath without a partner. A friend of hers did join them for short periods but basically she had little help - except, of course, when Rika, who was now living elsewhere, took over at weekends. Conditions of occupancy within Prairie Housing, and other aspects of the co-op, had gone awry of late and there was unusually little assistance forthcoming from the people who were now in the upstairs apartments in the house. I feel Irene has been gracious in referring in her letter only to her relationship with Catherine.

Cheryl at l'Avenir knew a woman who had once worked with some of our members and who was returning to Winnipeg that fall, 1992, so she contacted her when Irene said she had to leave Cath. Lynell and Brian (Mennonites again: they've been a Godsend in Catherine's life!) had spent three years studying in a seminary in Indiana and both were now qualified as church ministers. They were on the lookout for a parish in Manitoba where they could be hired as a team. They were happy to live with Cath in the interim and this also gave us breathing space in which to help Cath find more permanent roommates.

As it had been with Irene, it was a peaceful few months and Cath was very contented. Brian was a professional cook on the side and I was invited to several excellent meals with him and Lynell and Cath. It soon transpired that Lynell's creative instincts had been directed towards parenthood, so hers and Brian's need to find a job became increasingly urgent as her midriff expanded. Luckily a small country parish decided to welcome them for the beginning of

1993, just prior to when the baby was due, so while they made their plans we at l'Avenir made ours around Cath. Lynell contributed an interesting and succinct note to Cath's story:

Living with Cath improved our marriage! My own life has been enriched by my encounters with people with disabilities. In our time with Cath, Brian also had the opportunity for the growth that inevitably happens when a person opens their lives to a Catherine. It was good for me to watch, and it gave us, as a couple, a new common experience and language.

AGMs and Other Gigs

Thanks to Cath I've travelled widely (even to Australia for a glorious month in 1992) since **Does She Know She's There?** was published. I've always enjoyed these speaking engagements - gigs - but early on learned to expect surprises.

Soon after the book's[4] emergence, I was asked to speak at the Annual General Meeting of a local branch of ACL in a small Ontario town. I anticipated about fourteen people at the meeting, mainly parents like myself, with the addition of a service provider or two.

The lone disembarking passenger, I clambered out of the plane, looked both ways and crossed the tarmac to the terminal - a shed with two doors marked In and Out - and wondered if there were any buses into town. I was staying at a motel, which was also the site of the meeting. I was surprised when a charming fellow, all smiles, approached me and took my arm. "Hi there," he said, "I won the draw to pick you up!"

"Well thank you," I murmured as he led me from the shed across an expanse of muddy ruts to his car, "But the bus - "

"Bus! You think we'd let you take the bus? Careful now, we don't want you tripping and hurting yourself." Solicitousness personified, he helped me into the car. Suspecting by now that the AGM was a bigger deal than I thought, I asked how many people were expected.

"How many? Lady, I got four hundred guys with their tongues hanging out waiting to see you this evening." Steering with one hand, he waved the other in the air. "How 'bout that, eh? Hey," he added while my brain turned somersaults, "I'm Fred, by the way. Guess I was too excited to introduce myself."

I took his proffered hand. "And of course I'm Nicola," I responded with a gracious smile.

It was Fred's turn to be puzzled. "Nicola," he said with a frown. "That your private name, then?"

"Private? It's my only name...well, that and Schaefer." Fred's smile vanished and he released my hand abruptly.

"You mean," he said with horror mounting on his face, "you mean you're not Brandy the exotic dancer?" I shook my head regretfully and the car veered onto the verge and stopped.

Horror became panic in Fred. "But you were the only one that got off the plane...you gotta be Brandy...and that was the last plane in today and...oh my God. Oh my God, I don't believe this."

I asked Fred what his men's club was paying Brandy and he asked me when my meeting was over and we nearly came to an arrangement but I hadn't brought my feather fans. There were fourteen people at my meeting and I had a unique ice-breaker.

I'm always fascinated to hear other parents' stories and also to spend time with people who have disabilities and who can be powerful advocates for themselves and for others. I seldom come home without useful information or a good idea. I recall years ago bumping into a friend of Cath's and mine, Judith, who uses a wheelchair. She looked somehow different, better than when I'd last seen her but I couldn't identify why. I said as much to her but she only grinned and told me I had to work it out for myself. I couldn't, so she looked down at her lap tray. It was see-through plexi-glass and barely noticeable. That was the point, and I realized that the last time I'd seen her it had been in a solid colour.

As soon as I got home I ordered a plexi-glass tray for Cath to replace the vinyl covered wooden one she'd had for years. The difference was astonishing; one saw her as a whole person rather than as a top and a pair of legs. I think she appreciated being able to look down and see her legs and feet, specially since she now knew when to warn whoever was pushing her, by tensing up, not to catch her foot going round a corner in the house. In my slide show I have pictures of her with both kinds of tray and someone often comes up afterwards and says what a good idea.

I try when I'm talking about Catherine's life,

particularly her current living situation, to stress that the arrangement we've helped her concoct shouldn't be treated as a recipe. To carry the cooking analogy further, we knew that the basic ingredients for Cath had to be a good place to live, friends who valued her, the opportunity to pursue activities she enjoyed and fundamental security. I would think these would be the basics when planning anyone's life with or for them but, as with any good cooking, one changes some of the ingredients and their amounts in recipes according to taste and availability.

In other words, Cath's situation works for her; in Winnipeg; at the moment. But it might change, and it would have been quite different had Cath herself been a different person. I get colossal satisfaction from hearing, when I return to a city a couple of years after speaking there for the first time, that Cath's story ignited people's imaginations and led to similar arrangements to hers being set up where until that time there had only been what are sometimes known as cookie-cutter six-bed group homes or, in beer-drinking country, six-packs.

Conferences are useful events at which to exchange ideas, be inspired, embark and elaborate on friendships, laugh, cry and, last but not least, get caught up on the latest terminology around disability. Recently a keen student asked me the politically correct way to describe my daughter. "Catherine," I said but then relented and we discussed the issue.

When Catherine was small the terms used about her here in Canada were mentally retarded and crippled, yet when I took her to England they became

mentally handicapped and spastic. Later, here, she
was labelled, at various times, developmentally
delayed (implying, I always felt, that, like a train,
she would eventually catch up and reach her
destination), neurologically impaired and not too
swift. I rather liked the last one, since it could apply
to most of us in at least one aspect of our lives. For a
while 'differently-abled' did the rounds but luckily
didn't take hold; we're constantly striving to help
people with disabilities be recognized as more rather
than less similar to everyone else and that term
merely reinforced the difference. Now, of course, the
trendy word is 'challenged', so Cath has intellectual
and physical challenges. The trouble with this and
other well-intentioned terms is that they soon develop
quotation marks around them and become jokey.
Our friend Chris Dafoe, for instance, who happens
not to be tall, wrote a very funny article recently
about being vertically challenged.

The first time I spoke in public about Cath was in
the late '70s at a big weekend gathering in Quebec
generated by the Canadian Association for Community
Living (CACL) and involving parents and other
activists from across Canada. I introduced myself as
the mother of a severely multiply handicapped
daughter called Catherine. Afterwards another
mother, Audrey, from whom I've since learned so
much, gently remonstrated with me. "You have a
daughter called Catherine who has severe multiple
disabilities," she said. I got the message and ever
since, when necessary, have referred to Catherine as
a person who has disabilities, rarely even shortening

it by saying she's disabled. At that meeting I also met Barb Goode, one of Canada's leading advocates for people who are intellectually challenged (or whatever term is in fashion when this is read). "I'm a person first," says Barb, "and I don't like being labelled." "Label jars, not people" is the motto of the organization she helped to found, People First. It was also she and other members of People First, incidentally, who lobbied for years to have the Canadian Association for the Mentally Retarded (CAMR) changed to the Canadian Association for Community Living (CACL).

Dangers

By nature an optimist, I find it easy when I'm speaking at conferences to get so caught up in the numerous positive aspects of Cath's life, and the many good things that have happened in Winnipeg for people with disabilities, that I sometimes gloss over the difficulties we've experienced en route.

One of the key words that's written on the tattered sheet of notes I keep on hand when I'm rabbiting on is "dangers." I've already referred to one of my concerns, that of making Cath's housing arrangement sound like a recipe. Another thing I try to avoid is making things sound too simple. Examples of this are the workings of Prairie Housing Cooperative (PHC) and l'Avenir co-operatives. PHC very nearly collapsed a few years ago.

There were several reasons for this. Firstly, other than the apartment block, the clusters of houses are scattered all over Winnipeg, allowing the co-op members to become isolated from each other. The proportion of people with disabilities has at times risen to almost 40%, mainly because people with disabilities receive a rent subsidy, and the membership has been preoccupied with finances (sometimes to the exclusion of community considerations).

Secondly, there have been, at times, disagreement and lack of interest in the co-op as a co-op, i.e. many members weren't interested in playing their part in running it, and the few people who did play an active role tended to burn out.

Finally and most importantly, there have been periods of plain bad management. I believe the most significant overall reason for the co-op's difficulties was that although the original concept was clearly defined, some safeguards for ensuring people's commitment had not been defined at all. To put it crassly, this meant that if a person moved in and proved to be a lousy neighbour there was no way of getting rid of her or him unless it was purely a matter of the rent not being paid. The problems Prairie Housing Coop had run into have now being addressed but they could have been avoided.

Problems we've encountered in l'Avenir have been of a different nature and have nearly always been due to inadequate funding. It may sound odd, and indeed is, but the Government provides more funding to people living in group homes/community residences than it does to those who are living singly or in pairs. This means that if Cath lived with, say, three other people with disabilities she and l'Avenir would both be considerably better off financially. Since most of l'Avenir's members live in Cath-like situations, we're much poorer than agencies who serve people mainly in group homes. Heaven knows, this disparity has been pointed out enough times to the (Conservative) Government policy makers but we've yet to see any significant improvement.

One of the most maddening aspects of this conundrum is that we can afford to pay our staff far less than they would make if they were working in group homes, let alone St. Amant or the big institution - and for far more demanding work. We consider we're providing a vastly superior, individualized service to our members to that which they'd receive in an institution but on a paltry budget. What's more, funding for people with disabilities living in community has been **frozen** since 1989, while the cost of living in Manitoba has increased by **26%** in that same period.

Another danger I need to be aware of is implying that Cath's household has been all love and laughter for the last eleven years. Most of the time the house has run according to the original plan and the atmosphere has been truly joyful and co-operative. But, as is true of any large family or mixed household, there have been periods of acrimony between members and occasionally a person has moved in who has initially appeared to be co-op minded but who has ultimately created serious problems. However, these matters are not insuperable and were I to be embarking on a new living situation for Cath today I would probably choose the same basic plan.

What does she do during the day?

What does she do during the day? This question naturally crops up when I'm talking about Catherine's life. I think I know what she'd *like* to do from Monday to Friday: she'd like to have two people, a man and a woman, both of whose company she enjoyed, at her service all day. They would appear at her door at 9.00 a.m. and, depending on her state of health and her mood, would either stay at home with her or go with her for a jaunt in the van. If it was an at-home day because she was unwell, these people would do whatever they could to help her feel comfortable. If she appeared interested in staying home for some reason other than illness, her friends would entertain her in whatever way appealed to her.

They might read to her, play her electronic keyboard with her (she's pretty good at picking out notes with her left hand), look at magazines with her, leap around, dance wildly to loud music, fall off or over the furniture (including her bed, with her in it), swing her around in her wheelchair, get into the Jacuzzi with her, give her massages, and so on. (It would be necessary, incidentally, for the two people with Cath to be slightly eccentric and very imaginative). If it was a going-out day the trio might go swimming, to a movie, to the park, on a shopping spree, to visit friends or anything else that took their fancy - all with frequent coffee and food breaks. Or the day might be a combination of going out and staying home. The key would be flexibility.

That's the dream. Reality, of course, is different.

When Project Inclusion concluded after three years
(it lost much of its funding but has recently been
revived in a slightly different form and for a different
group of students) Cath joined a daytime program
for some fifteen people with complex disabilities.
The people running this program would like nothing
more than to be able to provide the sort of personalized
day described above for every one of the participants.
The problem, it need hardly be said, is funding.

Most social agencies in Manitoba are expected to
provide a 'day program' on a wretched $22.00 per
person per day to people who have a disability and
who are unable to compete in the job market. As a
result of hefty lobbying over the years by l'Avenir
and the folks running the program Cath's in, she
and the other participants don't do badly compared
to some, but they could, of course, do much better.
The program is based in a couple of ordinary offices -
with bathroom and kitchen facilities - in a small
strip mall next to my bank and local drugstore. The
aim is to spend as little time as possible in the offices
but, rather, to have everyone out and about.

Cath is picked up by one of several local transportation
firms designed for people with disabilities and on
Mondays, Wednesdays and Fridays she arrives at
the program by 9.30. Weather permitting, mornings
are usually spent visiting local stores and coffee
shops or walking around the neighbourhood. After
lunch, whatever the weather, she and a couple of
other participants and assistants get picked up by
bus and go downtown to swim - or, in Cath's case,
happily float on her back and kick - in the pool at the

spanking new "Y". A friend phoned me recently to say that one day she was in a downtown skywalk and found herself looking down at the "Y" pool: "There were three women getting out of the pool," she said. "They seemed to be helping one another, working together, and the effect was that of a choreographed ballet sequence in slow motion. It was beautiful, and I watched, fascinated, until they were on dry land. And then I suddenly realized that one of the women was Catherine - being helped by the other two."

Until recently, on Tuesdays and Thursdays Cath got picked up and taken directly to Body Sculpture where she met an assistant from the program and, with other men and women in search of a more fit physique, spent an hour having different parts of her body moved around on padded tables that function electronically. This form of passive exercise was invented for people who have had polio but able-bodied people get their workout by pushing against whatever the table is doing. For example, if the top half of the table is sitting the person up and down, he or she will try to do the opposite. When I discovered this form of exercise years ago, courtesy of Kevin, a core member of l'Arche, I took Cath to see if she'd like it. Two businessmen in suits and shiny shoes with bows on them lay on the tables next to her. As their legs were scissored back and forth and they fought the machine with agonized expressions, they had a discussion about the stock market. Catherine, who loves limbs flying round, nearly fell off the table giggling and blowing raspberries. Recently, together

with the folks at the day program, Sherill, who is
now Cath's live- in helper, organized an alternative
to Body Sculpture - physio and fun at the Re-Fit Centre - which is proving very successful.

Another daytime pursuit that Cath enjoyed for a
while was volunteering, with assistance, at a day
nursery a couple of days a week. She loves babies
and children and I like showing a slide of her as she
looks down with a maternal expression at a little boy
who is showing her a drawing he's done. Elke, who
was often the assistant who accompanied Cath to
the nursery, ultimately noticed, however, that her
friend had become disenchanted with the nursery
and spent much of the time there sleeping, so they
stopped going. We realized later that this was the
time when Cath's health problems had started, and
that she was probably sleeping due to exhaustion
from pain rather than boredom with the children.

Elke was a constant in Cath's life for many years
after Cath's move to her own home and was far more
than just a staff person in the day program. She
was, for instance, one of the first people to trek down
to the hospital when Catherine was there and was a
frequent dropper-in to her house. She has moved on
in her life now, but this is what she wrote a while
ago when I asked her about her relationship with
Cath:

> *When I first met Catherine in 1987 I didn't
> know how to be a friend to her. I had never met
> someone with a disability before and it was not an
> easy road. Cath was very unresponsive at first; she*

hardly ever smiled and when I got too close to her she always pushed me away. I felt that she disliked me in the beginning but I wasn't about to give up.

Cath turned me into a determined and patient person. Slowly but surely, through long walks and talks, we became closer. The first time she laughed at me it made my day. I had a hard time getting her jacket on her and was getting really frustrated but Cath got a real kick out of it. From then on things got much better. We started to build a close friendship, with Cath letting me know with gestures and expressions when she was in pain, felt ill or when she was happy and content. One day a couple of years after we'd met we were waiting for the bus after swimming. I was at a real low point and Cath must have caught on to this because all of a sudden I felt her pulling me towards her. She tried to comfort me by giving me a hug. It was the best day of my life!

Over the years I've been with Cath I've seen her grow happier and more communicative. She's taught me so much and has helped me realize that I can overcome obstacles. The other day we were swimming again and Cath was in such a great mood. We kept watching all the guys walking by and rating them. She turned up her nose at the ones she didn't like and put on her most charming smile for the gorgeous ones. We had a great time.

Cath and I have come a long way. We're real friends.

Cath volunteering at the day nursery

Swimming with Icelandic Sue

England

When Cath moved into her house I started going to England every summer. Harry, my dear stepfather, died in June 1987. I had visited him in the nursing home hours before his death and my mother and a friend and I were in the pub when my brother Edgar, who had visited his father just after me, phoned the pub with the news. I bought Mum a large gin and tonic and then told her. She sat absolutely still for a moment and then said firmly, "Good. He'd suffered enough. Good." The nurses in the home, and the patients, always enjoyed it when Harry turned up in old films on TV and one of the nurses told me later about the last moments of his life: " He was an actor to the end, was Harry. He had the heroin, dear, so he wasn't suffering. I asked him if he'd like a sip of his whisky and he nodded. I helped him with it and afterwards he smiled and said, 'thank you, that was lovely' and then he was gone."

Harry had been ill for years and Mum had, in her own caring but sometimes brusque way, looked after him. She missed him sorely and became terrified of growing incapacitated herself. To ward off her fears she continued to swim in the pool over at Greatham, to don her men's gumboots and keep the garden more or less under control and, picking up where she'd left off years before, to attend painting classes and create oil paintings with a fierce intensity.

The day I arrived the summer after Harry died, an elegantly attired woman came picking her way carefully down the steep, uneven path to the cottage in high-heeled shoes. She was carrying a foil-covered tray. "Ah," said my mother, "here comes Meals on Heels.'" She had always disliked cooking and this was her one concession to old age.

It was an awful shock when, in May 1990, my mother died instantaneously from a cerebral hemorrhage. She was eighty-two and until her death had been as mentally and physically vital as ever. She had, however, been saying for at least a year that she wanted to die. We'd tended to brush this off but maybe she knew something we didn't. At any rate, we were glad for her that she had done it the way she wanted - suddenly, with no fuss.

Dominic was living back in Winnipeg at this time so he and I flew over and joined Ben, who had been living in Oxford for two years, and the rest of Mum's descendants at the cottage. It was the first time ever that we'd all been together - my sister Veronica, her son Richard and daughter Eleanor and their partners and children, my brother Edgar, myself and the boys. The only person missing, unfortunately, was Cath, but it would have been well-nigh impossible to take her over to England.

Between us we organized a simple but good memorial service in the nearby country church of Mum's childhood. A cousin arranged wild flowers in wine carafes on the altar, a touch we knew Cordelia would have enjoyed, and Dominic and Ben dragged our ancient audio system to the church and everyone trooped out after the service to some of Mum's favourite Louis Armstrong numbers. At the cottage afterwards about eighty friends and relatives of all ages, some with white hair and others with dreadlocks, came from near and far for a celebration of her life that continued until breakfast the next day. We decked the cottage and garden, which was a glory of flowers and nesting birds, with her paintings, one of which she had finished days before and with which she was particularly pleased. I think everyone had trouble realizing she wasn't, as she would normally have been, sitting on a piece of old sacking by her bonfire with a homemade cigarette in her hand and a gin by her side on the grass.

Nothing gives me more pleasure than going to England each year and spending time with Ben and the rest of our England family. We've managed to hang on to the cottage and for the last few years Ben, with a small gang of cousins and friends, has made it his home. He's also its caretaker; the place being about six hundred years old, this is a considerable responsibility. In the spring of '97, he completely redid the roof, i.e. removed over eight thousand tiles, replaced rotten or deathwatch beetle-infested beams and then put the tiles back. He also knocked two small rooms downstairs into one and put up a magificent support beam between the two. It was fashioned from an ash tree he'd felled for the purpose three years previously.

After attending a nearby agricultural college and a number of carpentry courses, he seems to have found his calling as a man of the land, and a builder/re-storer. He seems contendedly dug in but does admit to the odd bout of homesickness, so I either send or take over Canadian care packages - Hudson's Bay underwear, 'real' sweat pants, peanut butter cups, Turtles and other candy, books about Winnipeg and photos of Cath, about whose life he always wants every detail. It pleases me that he has made friends with some of the members of the l'Arche community in nearby Bognor Regis and welcomes them to the cottage for time off and a change of scene.

He came to see for himself how Cath was in the summer of 1995. After sending over his motorbike (utilitarian, fast but not fancy) in four massive parcels he appeared on the doorstep, put the thing together and spent several weeks with us, doing tree work in the neighbourhood (he brought his saws, harness and ropes), spending time with Cath and whitewater rafting in the wilds of Ontario with childhood friends. Then he piled his gear onto and hanging down the sides of his motorbike and brrrmed off to explore the Rockies and thence to see Dominic in Vancouver.

Dominic found his calling way back in 1986 when he first went to England. It's photography. He'd been acting suspiciously for some time before he left, spending hours - sometimes days - arranging a feather on top of a broom against the back wall of the house and photographing it from all angles and in all lights. When he returned from Europe after two years he sequestered Ben's room and transformed it into a darkroom. Some stunning prints of Sussex emerged from that period and are still among his best. In 1990 he spent a year at a photography school in Victoria and then moved to Vancouver to live.

In August 1993 he had his first gallery show and

Ted encouraged me to fly out. Seeing sixteen of our son's black and white prints, each one beautiful in its own right, arranged on three sides of a simple but attractive gallery, was a moving experience. I also enjoyed basking in reflected glory as his friends and admirers approached me and asked if I was really Dominic's mother. I was far less modest in my response than was Dominic as he received congratulations.

Since then he's been the photographer for a business magazine. Because, like his father, he's a perfectionist where work is concerned, this occupies much of his time but he's managed to make quite a name for himself simply as an excellent photographer/artist on the side.

Like his brother, he always wants to know how Cath is and I recently, at his request, named him a trustee of the fund in her name in my Will.

Winnipeg in the 1990's

For the last few years Ted and I have lived eight blocks, or a good dog walk, apart. We're on very good terms. We share news about our children's lives and our own (after thirty-nine years of hard slogging away at the University, he retired, joyfully, in the spring of '97), and exchange books and magazines. We also often meet at Catherine's house at get-togethers, and other family events. He lives in our old house and I'm in the lower two floors of a huge old house, similar to Cath's, and have friends living in a separate apartment upstairs. I have official sleeping spots in my part for six visitors, plus floor space and mattresses, so friends from the two main sides of my life, music and the disability field, can and do come to stay.

About two hundred and sixty people have bedded down here so far, some for a night, some for up to six months and others on a weekly basis. This last group includes l'Arche assistants; living in l'Arche is not always a heavenly experience and these young people desperately need a place where they can collapse and regenerate. I consider myself fortunate to be able to provide a bolt-hole. One summer at Folk Festival time I had a nine-piece brass band from New York, hotly followed by the Oyster Band (six blokes) from England, hotly followed by Friends in High Places - brilliant stilt dancers from Manhattan. Somewhere in all of this music and dance Sister Mary, a nun connected with l'Arche in Syracuse, spent a night or two with us. I love all this and the gains are immeasurable. Ted, a self-confessed hermit, shudders when I tell him about it. He says he prefers books for company.

Providentially, my house already had a ramp, so Catherine and others can visit easily. I have her old hospital bed in 'her' room in my house and she has a nifty one at her place that I bought secondhand from a hospital for $200. It goes up and down, sits her up or raises her knees at the touch of a button and is a great success, particularly with visiting children. People of all heights attend to Cath's needs when she's on her bed and over the years, several have developed sore backs because the bed is either too high or too low. A useful aspect of this bed is that the whole thing can be raised or lowered, again electronically.

at Darlene's wedding ...

One of the happy events Ted and I attended together was Darlene's wedding in the summer of 1991. Catherine was present too, of course, looking rather thin and wan because she was still recovering from her big operation, but happy nonetheless. Darlene had been teaching up north for two years and we had missed her. She and her husband Greg live in town now and they visit back and forth with Cath, as well as with Ted and myself. I feel a satisfying sense of continuity about the fact that seven years ago I pursuaded Darlene to join l'Avenir's Board and she even spent three years as our super conscientious President.

In July 1993 Ted and I dropped by Cath's house to help her celebrate her thirty-second birthday.

"The garden looks good," said Ted, nervously jovial, "look at all those tomato plants."

"And I've never seen such a profusion of flowers here," I said, "the ramp's almost invisible. Come on!"

There were crowds of people there and as I sorted through them the sense of continuity that I feel about Darlene's eleven year friendship with Cath expanded as I realized that many of the people making music and swilling beer on my daughter's front deck or talking inside the house had been in her life almost as long as Darlene and in some cases longer. The Dafoes were there, as were Evelyn and Marie, David, Elke, Rika, Cheryl, Rod, Dave and several others including friends from l'Avenir. Assisting Cath to welcome people were Keith and Kathleen, her roommates since the beginning of that year. Many of their friends were also at the party.

Cath and I first met this singular couple in my sittingroom when Cath was staying with me for Christmas in 1992. Along with Rika, who insisted, rightly, on being present as Cath's friend and advocate, we were conducting informal interviews with a number of people who thought they might like to move in with Cath when Lynell and Brian left in February. Cath, as so often when I wished she would be in an alert and beguiling mood, sat there looking completely blah throughout each interview and it struck me for the umpteenth time that a person immobilized and speechless in a wheelchair often has no choice in where they're plonked and who they meet. Maybe Cath didn't want to be there that day. Interestingly, when I asked Kathleen recently about her initial impression of Catherine she described her as a magnet. "I was drawn to her immediately - it was an almost physical tug. I just knew I wanted to be around her, get to know her, be part of her life."

Kathleen was twenty-two at the time - a lovely, sensitive, practical young woman. She has an outstanding gift for creating beauty wherever she goes. One of the things that warmed me to her immediately was her response to my question regarding doing Cath's personal care. Would it bother her, I wondered? Well yes, she said, it would, because Catherine would surely feel it was an invasion of her privacy to have a strange woman washing her. But, Kathleen added, she would be as respectful as she knew how. Keith was forty-two and had a wealth of experience in many areas of life, including taxi-driving, managing a bakery and working with people who have disabilties. The latter, he says, are the only jobs where he has felt truly fulfilled. His upright bearing, somewhat stern look and blunt words belie a sensitivity equal to Kathleen's. They had been together - not always, they freely admitted, without difficult periods - for five years and intended to remain so. Rika and I, with a few reservations (they really were unusual), liked them, and Cath did grant Keith a small chuckle when he carefully helped her with her tea. Keith and I had several friends in common and he encouraged me to ask them for character references. I got the same response from all of them. In summary, it was that Keith was hardworking, 100% honest and reliable, and once he'd decided to be one's friend there was nothing he wouldn't do for one. And Kathleen? A beautiful personality - bright, too. And as a couple? They were devoted to each other and complemented one another well; a great team. Would they be good for Cath? Absolutely.

L'Avenir's recently installed new general manager, (Cheryl had left to teach at Red River Community College) was Bob, who had been on the Association for Community Living (ACL) Winnipeg's board at the same time as I had and was head of Red River's audio/visual department. He had the final say in who would be hired and, after checking out Keith's work references, allowed himself to be persuaded by my gut feeling that Keith and Kathleen would be the right people for Catherine. He now acknowledges that I have reliable guts.

Lynell and Brian and Rika between them helped Kathleen and Keith become more closely acquainted with Cath and I was allowed to put in my two cents' worth. Rika, Cath and I had been invited to participate in an ACL family conference in Edmonton at the beginning of February, which gave Lynell and Brian time to move out and Keith and Kathleen to move in. It was years since I'd travelled by plane with Cath. It's a tricky business and involves transferring her from her wheelchair to the plane seat with little maneuvering space. I automatically went into my organizing mode and started making one conflicting suggestion after another as more passengers started queuing up behind us. Rika stopped me in mid-muddle and organized the move with quiet efficiency.

The conference was in the Fantasyland hotel, which is attached to the Edmonton mall. Rather than one of the 'theme' rooms which Rika had pushed for we had, instead, a huge room with a Jacuzzi. Catherine, relieved to have arrived somewhere, lay on a bed and looked around the room with wide eyes. Rika, the kid in her suddenly emerging (I kept forgetting how young she was), went around bouncing on the king-sized beds, investigating the basket of 'free' toiletries in the bathroom, lying in the empty Jacuzzi and looking at herself in the ceiling mirror ("Cath, you'll love this!") and squeaking with delight at each new discovery, ("Hey Nicola, get a load of this mini-bar!") Later, we got Cath into her wheelchair and the two of them charged off to explore the mall. They returned hours later armed with such essentials as four massive bottles of Diet Coke (for Rika - she appeared to live on the stuff), tea-making equipment (for Cath and myself) and bag upon bag of life-threatening snacks - chips, candy - for all of us. There was also a bright red Speedo swimsuit for Cath. I winced at the colour. "She chose it," said Rika, "it's not the colour I liked but it was the one she kept pointing at." And actually, she looked pretty good in it as we floated in the Jacuzzi later.

When we got back to Cath's apartment it had been transformed. Unlike most of their predecessors, Keith and Kathleen had a significant amount of furniture and other possessions and they had integrated their stuff tastefully with Catherine's. One of the most striking new aspects of the place was the sudden abundance of greenery, which hung from the ceilings, spilled over the edges of shelves and was draped over doorways. Cath now also had fresh herbs growing in a tray on her windowsill - "I thought she might enjoy the aroma," said Kathleen - and a large fern curled down from the shelf over her bed . Hanging on a string from the same shelf was a fantasmagorical winged creature made for Cath by Kathleen from bright material and studded with beads and bits of mirror - "It must get pretty boring just looking up at a plain old shelf." She had spent time in the Middle East as a child and the apartment now reflected this with adroitly placed exotica - a hand woven rug on the wall here, an inlaid table there and other smaller items - brass pots, candlesticks, dishes - everywhere.

Kathleen is a whiz with a sewing machine and had already made extra cushions for Cath's sofa and was now working on much-needed new curtains for the sittingroom. She'd also made me a present; being an orderly woman, and having noticed the mess around my telephone table, she'd used some leftover cushion cover material to sew me a sort of mini-wall hanging with separate pouches for my pens, notepad and glasses. It's invaluable. Keith is almost as keen a reader as Ted, so there were now several additional bookcases and shelves around the place and, since he's also a musician, a variety of music-making equipment.

His carpentry materials were stacked neatly in

Three beautiful women
Kathleen, Cath and friend Monica

the basement along with his overflow of books. Ever
since Glen's and Laurie's time there had been cats in
the apartment and Keith and Kathleen carried on
the tradition by bringing their two. One was peering
out nervously from behind an arrangement of
Keith's antique tins on a shelf in the kitchen and the
other was already curled up on Cath's bed. Added to
all this visual beauty and coziness, Keith was baking
bread, so there was a marvellous smell filling the
kitchen.

Apart from some illness the following year was a
really good one for Catherine. She was demonstrably
happy with Kathleen and Keith, who really loved

her and provided a fine combination of stability and
entertainment. The apartment always looked, smelled
and felt beautifully welcoming and there were
frequent parties - Jacuzzi and otherwise - which
always included music provided by Keith and his
friends. At least two of his and Kathleen's friends
told me how much they appreciated being able to
visit them without being hauled up flights of bloody
stairs in their wheelchairs. The great advantage
about parties at home, for Cath, is that if she gets
fed up she can retreat to her room.

Rika Remembers

Cath and Rika

People often dropped in. One of these was Rika, who was now in the bachelor apartment upstairs. When she quit as Cath's weekend helper, she thought I'd be upset but the letter she wrote about her relationship with Cath explains why I wasn't:

> *Catherine is a teacher, but this ability of hers is separate from who she is as a person. The lessons she's taught me are from being around her and having to adjust and broaden my perceptions about communication, language and friendship.*
>
> *I never felt very close to Cath until after the first year of our being together, when the worst of her illness was over. That was when I got to see*

the part of her that Nicola, Sonja and many others had told me about, the part of Cath that is happy, full of life and spirit, the part of Cath that was able to give to me in many touching and wonderful ways. While she was ill I saw a great deal of the pain that she went through and was often the only person she could show it to. She let me know very clearly that she was hurting and I often mistook this as personal dislike for me. I realize now that she was communicating with me the only way she knew how and that I wasn't picking up very well on what she had to say.

With Cath my dependence on words has lessened. I needed to understand how unnecessary words are before I could let go of trying to build our friendship on what I said with them. I had to realize we weren't going to have a close relationship unless we were on equal ground, and we gradually achieved this through living together and sharing numerous life experiences. Many people see Cath as being limited in what she can say because she doesn't use words, but I feel quite the opposite. I can't use words to say half of what I'd like to because I'm using this medium to communicate about a friend who I don't think of in these terms.

Between Cath and I, language has become an experience of touch, sight and sound. Our shared enthusiasm for sound and music has been one of the building blocks of our friendship. Some of our most intimate moments have been while at a concert, participating in a drumming circle or while on the back porch at dusk listening to the birds. Often,

*our hands will join in the darkness and between
them a dance will take form, creating a tangible
link between us and the music around us.*

*We're at a point now where we don't deal with
the details of each other's daily lives and our time
together is spent enjoying each other's company. I
stopped working with Cath because I didn't want
to be paid to be a friend and it's important to me
that I spend time with her because I want to, because
our time together is what we've chosen to give each
other.*

*In Catherine I have a friend who touches me in
a place that others rarely do, a place that's usually
vulnerable and hidden. When I think of her and
my relationship with her I think of how I feel
around her, about touching hands and about the
things she says with her eyes that no-one could
ever say to me with words. I think about the love
between us and how precious it is to me, and about
how I don't think it would be there except for
Cath's abilities, as a teacher and as a friend.*

Another regular dropper-in was Icelandic Sue,
who worked in Cath's day program. She became a
close friend of both Cath's and her roommates and
was one of Cath's weekend helpers.

Catherine had a bad spell in the fall of 1993.
Keith and Kathleen, with tireless dedication, saw
her through a couple of chest infections but, as she
had in her pre-operation days, she was also experiencing bouts of severe pain for no obvious reason.
She had been so healthy of late that I'd forgotten she

was periodically supposed to have her esophagus checked and, if necessary, stretched. Keith and I took her to see Dr. T.H. and an X-ray showed that her left lung had collapsed. As she happened that day to be in excellent spirits and looking completely well, we were baffled.

During the subsequent investigation of her esophagus (it was fine) Dr. T.H. suctioned out the top part of the lung (the only area one can get at, apparently) and pumped it full of air. However, when Keith took her to the hospital a few days later because she was in extreme pain, another X-ray revealed that it was once again flat. While we sat there wondering what to do Cath suddenly cheered up, started accepting a few sips of water and was plainly ready to go home, flat lung or not. It was puzzling.

Dr. T.H. suggested I consult a respiratory specialist about Catherine. This doctor said that, due to her scoliosis, which bends her to the left, that lung was constantly being compressed and would probably never fully reinflate. He didn't think the condition would cause her to be in pain. I asked what we could do. "Aggressive physiotherapy," was the response, so that was what Keith and I promptly organized.

Jean, a splendid woman from a local Home Therapy team, started visiting Cath on a daily basis for a while and, through positioning and thumping and squeezing, got Catherine breathing more deeply. Keith quickly learned her techniques and he and Kathleen incorporated physio into Cath's daily life. Even with only one lung working well, Cath seems fine and my suspicion is that the other had quietly packed up long before it was noticed. Jean continues to work with Cath on a regular basis and has become a valued friend.

There are several issues I'd like to see addressed in Cath's life. When she was at school years ago she had been introduced to choice-making by means of electronic equipment. A while before she left home a friend had made her a gizmo that would allow her to turn her bedroom light on and off by remote control. It required her to flip a switch and, frankly, she either couldn't co-ordinate her hand to do this or else she wasn't interested. I now think I should have persevered with the idea. Also, she's never owned a powered wheelchair. My excuse - a lame one, I admit - for not having pursued this is that there always seem to be so many absolute necessities to attend to. And finally, we would all love it if we could find a way of helping Catherine communicate more easily. We've tried symbols and letter boards and various methods involving computers and other electronic machines, but none of these so far has helped her much, if at all.

In the meantime, she has become far more determined and successful about making her wishes known. This is due largely, I know, to the people around her since she left home having been extraordinarily sensitive to the way she communicates, but I'm not alone in thinking that she herself has found a way to transmit many more of her choices than she did when she was younger. I reckon she has made for herself a pretty good and at least partly self determined life.

Cath and Nicola in earnest discussion

A Decade of Success

On July 18th, 1986, days before her 25th birthday, Catherine moved from her parents' house into her own home on the ground floor of 822 Preston. It was an exciting, somewhat anxious time, the culmination of about two years of planning and hard work on the part of many people. Everyone had been eager to help Cath create a home for herself where she would have both the necessary paid, live-in support and the freely given friendship and help of others living in the two upstairs apartments. Could such a novel arrangement work?

In the succeeding years there have been wonderful times at 822 Preston, and many equally wonderful people have been - and in some cases still are - an important part of Catherine's life, and she of theirs. It hasn't always been perfect - what household is? - but we can now say that it not only could work, it has worked, and we hope and believe it will continue to do so.

Catherine invites you to help her celebrate her 35th birthday and the 10th anniversary of her move to her own place. She would also like you to meet her housemates, including Sherrill, her primary support person, who incidentally was already part of her life 10 years ago.

DATE: MONDAY 22ND JULY 1996

PLACE: 822 PRESTON
TIME: 6:00 ONWARD

The Party

Cath and some of her friends

It was a grand party. About fifty of Catherine's friends and former roommates ambled up the sloped path to her front door during the evening, many bearing gifts and foil-covered plates of good stuff to eat. A number who were unable to be there sent regrets and good wishes. There was much music and laughter and storytelling, particularly of the "Hey, do you remember -" variety as events around Cath's life in her house were recalled. Ted was there and provided a foam box loaded with beer and wine. Darlene made the birthday cake. A good friend, John, kindly lent us his professional services and videoed the whole event. Cath was beautiful if bemused throughout but, as is her custom after a hectic happy time, had a long reflective giggle in bed when everyone had gone.

One of the people helping her greet people was a long-time friend of ours, Sherrlll, more of whom shortly.

When, after two and a half good years with Cath, Keith and Kathleen moved into their own apartment nearby, their place with Cath was taken by Tracy, a young woman lately from Newfoundland. Tracy had a penchant for helping anyone or anything in trouble and during her time with Cath - during which Cath was both well and cheerful - I never knew who or what I would encounter when I visited: temporarily motherless children, temporarily childless mothers (during child custody embroglios) and permanently, until they found Tracy, homeless animals.

Unfortunately, Tracy developed serious health problems and had to leave Catherine sooner than any of us had anticipated. What happened next is best described by Cath's current room-mate, Sherrill.

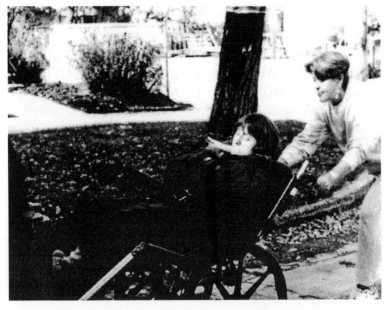

Sherrill helping Cath into her van - 1997

Sherrill's Experiences with Catherine

In July 1986 I attended an extraordinary celebration - a house blessing for Catherine Schaefer. Like many young women of 25, Catherine was setting up her own household but, because she was unable either to walk or speak, her family, with the creative assistance of David Wetherow, had designed a unique situation for her. Cath's new home was a lovely white older home, three storeys high, embellished by a curving wheelchair ramp leading to a small deck at the back, a columned two-storey porch, several leaded glass windows and one of those roof ventilators that give a

*place the appearance of a Middle-Eastern mosque.
There was a warm gathering of friends and
Catherine's new housemates, and Catherine herself,
of course, as Father Eric Jensen processed through
the house sprinkling it amply with holy water, and
then we walked across the road to the park and
enjoyed a celebratory meal.*

*I remember shedding a few happy tears that
day, reflecting the happiness with which I was
surrounded. Although it made little sense at the
time, as I was then married to David Wetherow,
had three children and a full-time job with the
Department of Education, there was a part of me
that wished I was moving into this place as well;
something was happening here that I didn't quite
understand. Sitting on the fringe of all the activity
as I was, however, I merely wondered at the courage
of all the participants, including Darlene, Cath's
first roommate.*

*I had first met Catherine at a New Year's Eve
party at the Schaefer family home some time before.
She had been enjoying all kinds of wonderful foods
when she unfortunately got something jammed in
her esophagus. I helped Nicola remove the spine-
supporting corset Catherine was wearing but I
remember my awkwardness and fear that I would
unintentionally do more harm than good. Something
about Cath made me want to come close but I
didn't know how to approach her. I watched the
warm ease with which Catherine's and Nicola's
friend Zana helped Cath but I remained in the dark.
There was no communication device and Catherine*

neither looked me in the eye nor relished my touch.

In 1991 David and I separated and three years later I moved into the upstairs apartment of Nicola's house with my two sons and a friend. Catherine came to visit quite often but although she joined us for various family celebrations with my children and Nicola, she and I made no strong connection until, with Nicola's permission, I practiced my newly acquired skill of Reiki with her. We sat quietly together watching television as I placed my hands in various positions on Cath's body. At first she only tolerated me, occasionally pushing my hands away, but as we sat in silence together over a period of several hours, a warm energy began to form between us. I needed this time alone with her to begin to establish a channel of communication - one without words. At Nicola's invitation, I began to visit Catherine in her own home. During these times I spoke little, continuing the Reiki experience and massaging the pressure points in her feet - a practice known as reflexology. Although I was often cold and tired as I went to her house I never failed to emerge from our sessions feeling happy and refreshed. When I first began massaging her feet, we both approached the experience with some caution. Due to her cerebral palsy, the muscles and tendons in her feet are often in spasm, so her feet are very tender. She often jumped or glared at me if I hit a sore spot, but with practice I learned to lighten my touch and she learned to relax and trust. I slowly added new forms of touch and found that she loves having her

*back muscles, legs, arms and hands massaged. I
massaged her spine timidly at first because it's
quite curved and I was afraid of hurting her, but
she soon began to experience a lot of release and
would deepen her breathing as I worked. The last
frontier was working on her head and neck. These
two, together with her left arm and hand, are the
areas of her body over which Cath has the greatest
control and she wasn't sure she wanted to "give"
them to me. She would sometimes allow me to
touch these areas briefly and then with a glare
push me away. We continued in this fashion for
about a year. Coming into her life in this limited
way, I had little awareness of just who she was,
how she lived her life.*

*In the spring of 1996, Catherine's roommate,
Tracy, announced that due to persistent personal
health problems she had decided to return to her
parents' home in Newfoundland. When Nicola told
me she was initiating a search for Tracy's replacement, I felt a resurfacing of the desire to move in
with Cath that had caught me by surprise ten
years earlier. I loved living upstairs in Nicola's
house, sharing so much of our lives, but the apartment
was too large for one person (the boys were leaving),
so I was reluctantly thinking about moving anyway.
I was hesitant to suggest myself to Nicola as Cath's
roommate; we are good friends and I didn't want
to put her on the spot.*

*Her very positive response lighted the way
through the following months. For one reason and
another, including my father's sudden death down*

in Virginia, my move into Catherine's house was very stressful and sometimes I felt I would collapse in exhaustion. It was in this private holocaust that I first began to truly know who Catherine is. One evening, as yet another thing went wrong, I fell on my knees beside her bed, crying. When I raised my head shamefully, Cath was looking at me with concern and as I moved near her, she reached out and stroked my head. It was in that moment that I knew how truly present she is to others. The opening between us widened in the ensuing days and I began to share with her what I was doing and feeling and to elicit her opinion on what she would prefer to do, eat or wear. I also began to read to her, something she seemed genuinely to enjoy. I wasn't sure how much she was actually under-standing but noticed that her reaction changed appropriately with the material content. At one point, while I was reading a poignant story that was particularly pertinent to our circumstances at the time, she began to laugh with a knowing look. I, too, began to laugh, and realized that we were indeed truly present to one another. I knew then my own definitive answer to the question Nicola had first posed with the title of her book.

The bonding process continues. It forms the basis of all the activities we pursue, making our lives together a joyful exploration of fresh possibility. This translates into simple things like making travel arrangements that leave her feeling animated rather than exasperated, or shopping together for a wardrobe that reflects her own coloring and personal taste, or being part of a women's drumming circle. We are also working together to create a communal universe in which each of us also has our own space. Catherine withdraws into herself when she needs to and so do I. I'm delighted when she chooses to emerge. And if I am not mistaken, she, too, rejoices in my returning.

When I'm alone with Catherine I feel truly free to play. She often initiates the mood by blowing raspberries, interspersed with hoots. Her beautiful eyes are large and animated with fun and delight at these times. I respond with sounds of my own, dancing and clowning around. She keeps me wound up with an increasing crescendo of noise and excited body springs. High on enthusiasm, she is rarely the one to terminate such sessions. We continue our personal sound symphonies in the car as we travel about. Sometimes, when she's tired of gadding about, she begins to intone the syllable 'home', obviously happy to be heading there. In the Jacuzzi, I began to put together our Reiki and sound sessions by placing my hands on the topside and underside of each of her chakras (energy centres) while chanting a sound traditionally associated with each. Since she loves to submerge her ears in the water, the sound vibration is travelling through both the water and my touch. I often make up my own songs at these times, sometimes with words and sometimes just a flow of babble. Her eyes shine and she joins me in experimenting with the sounds she can make. To date she has created four distinct "words" and is very pleased with herself.

One of Catherine's freedoms is that of being her own person. When she's tired she sleeps; when she's hungry she eats. Her face and body are true reflections of her state, unmasked by social expectations. In this she is my teacher and I am her slow student. I still eat when I'm full, smile when I'm in pain and generally ignore the signals my body sends me. I know that one of the quickest ways to heal myself when I'm unwell is to fast but I often fail to act on the knowledge. Catherine, however, tends to refuse any food when she's ill and she's usually the first in the household to finish with the current flu or cold virus.

Sages have written through the centuries about the art of living and loving simply. Catherine is the first person I have met who actually does those things. The gift of her presence is to allow those of us who are privileged to know her to experience just how simply loving and living is done. Were she to use words, she could say with complete candor, "I live simply as I am."

Everyone living at 822 Preston at the moment is community-spirited and pleased to be part of Cath's life. None of us knows how long this happy situation will last but I, for one, am heeding my daughter's example and rejoicing in the present.

Few biographies have a neat ending and my daughter's is no exception. Perhaps the best way to conclude this is to quote Margaret Meade:

> *If we are to achieve a richer culture,*
> *we must weave one in which*
> *each diverse human gift*
> *will find a fitting place.*

Catherine has helped us find many a fitting place for her gifts.

November 1997

1 Encouraged by the leadership of People First of Canada (an association of people who had lived and struggled with the label of mental retardation), the Canadian, Manitoba and Winnipeg Associations 'for the Mentally Retarded' were re-named 'Associations for Community Living'. In March, 1986, our local branch became the Association for Community Living - Winnipeg. CAMR Manitoba Division followed suit in May, and the National body became the Canadian Association for Community Living in October.

2 Many of the ideas that formed the inspiration for Catherine's home and support network are described in detail in **The Whole Community Catalogue**, an invaluable collection of ideas, stories, tools and connections for community living. In Canada, the book may be ordered from Inclusion Press, 24 Thome Cres., Toronto, M6H 2S5 Tel: 416-658-5363, Fax: 416-658-5067

US readers can order from Communitas, Box 374, Manchester, Connecticut 06040 ($18.00 postpaid).

3 **Does She Know She's There?**, Schaefer, Nicola, Fitzhenry and Whiteside, 1982.

4 **ibid**, Schaefer, Nicola

INCLUSION PRESS INTERNATIONAL
ORDER FORM

24 Thome Crescent
Toronto, ON   Canada M6H 2S5
Tel 416-658-5363 Fax 416-658-5067
E-mail: 74640.1124@compuserve.com

WEB PAGE: http://inclusion.com

v 1997 edition

Classic Videos

With a Little Help From My Friends
Prod: M. Forest & G. Flynn
The basics of creating schools where all kids belong and learn together. Hands on strategies – MAPS & Circles of Friends.

Kids Belong Together
Prod: People First Assoc of Lethbridge, Alta Featuring the late Fr. Patrick Mackan – a celebration of friendship – MAPS in action.

Together We're Better *Video*
Producer: Comforty Media Concepts
Staff Development Kit: a 2 hour video 3-pack of resources with Marsha Forest, Jack Pearpoint and Judith Snow demonstrating MAPS, PATH and CIRCLES. An inspiration.

Miller's MAP *Video*
Prod: Expectations Unltd &Inclusion Press
Children, parents, neighbors and professionals make inclusion happen– team facilitation and graphics in a MAP.

Friends of ...Clubs *Video*
Producers: Oregon Dept. of Education & University of Oregon A beautiful 15 min. story about creating community partnerships. Friends, friends, friends - the spark of life.

Dream Catchers *Video*
Producer: Institute on Disability, NH
New 16 minute video about dreams and circles of friends. Beautiful images, personal stories, images of the future. An inspiration.

PATH DEMONSTRATION Video
Producer: U. of Dayton, Inclusion Press
60 minute Path with a group of educators and parents. An excellent demonstration of Path problem solving in action with a team.

Inclusion News

The Center publishes an independent annual newspaper - articles & resources you need . It has raving fans! International flair. Order in volume - $50 for a box of 150. A Conference Must!

Inclusion Exclusion Poster
by Jack Pearpoint
A vibrant eye catching 18" X 24" graphic poster exploring the why behind Inclusion and Exclusion.

5th printing

Path: 2nd Edition
Planning Possible Positive Futures
Pearpoint, O'Brien, Forest
A guide to exciting, creative, colorful futures planning for families, organizations and schools to build caring "including" places to live, work & learn. Graphics unleash capacity. Path - an eight step problem solving approach involving dreaming and thinking backwards. Color graphic included!

3rd printing

The Inclusion Papers
Strategies to Make Inclusion Happen
Jack Pearpoint & Marsha Forest
Practical, down to earth and sensible. Perfect for conferences, courses and workshops. Circles of Friends, MAPS, articles about drop-outs, kids at risk, Medical School course and more... graphics, poetry, overheads...

What's Really Worth Doing
& How To DO IT! *by Judith Snow*   A book for people who love someone labeled disabled - possibly yourself. "This is a book of wisdom – an invitation to the dance of life." John McKnight

TheAll Star Company
Building   **People, Performance, Profit**
Teams   ★ ★ ★   *Nick Marsh* ★
An exciting book about BUILDING TEAMS and CHANGE. The All Star metaphor is about building powerful teams in your organization.

5th printing   **Action for Inclusion**
by *O'Brien and Forest* with Pearpoint, Snow & Hasbury
Over 20,000 copies distributed – "A down to earth blueprint of what 21st century education ought to be doing for all kids in regular classrooms. Powerful strategies for making it happen in a jargon-free, step-by-step book." Circles & MAPS Herb Lovett, Boston
L'Intégration en Action: Maintenant disponible en Français

From Behind the Piano
3rd printing
Building Judith Snow's Unique Circle of Friends
by *Jack Pearpoint*   afterword: *John O'Brien*
This is the story of Judith Snow & her Joshua committee. It demonstrates that love, determination and hard work will conquer challenges.   An inspiration for anyone struggling to make a difference.

Changes in Latitude/Attitude & Treasures
Two books from Inst. on Disability, NH
Changes: The Role of the Inclusion Facilitator - beautifully presented – the experience and wisdom of facilitators in New Hampshire.
Treasures: Photo essay on friendship - images of children in New Hampshire explains how to include everyone. Just do it.

INCLUSION PRESS ORDER FORM

24 Thome Crescent, Toronto, ON
Canada M6H 2S5
Tel 416-658-5363 Fax 416-658-5067
e-mail: 74640.1124@compuserve.com
WEB Page: http://inclusion.com

December 1997 Listing

Inclusion Press Books

		Copies	To
Path Workbook - 2nd Edition	$15 + $5 /1st copy shipping*	___	__
Planning Positive Possible Futures			
All My Life's a Circle	$15 + $5 /1st copy shipping*	___	__
New Expanded Edition- Circles, MAPS & PATH in Action			
When Spider Webs Unite	$15 + $5 /1st copy shipping*	___	__
Challenging Articles on Community & Inclusion by Shafik Asante			
Members of Each Other	$15 + $5 /1st copy shipping*	___	__
Collected Articles on Building Community & Friendship - O'Brien&Lyle O'Brien			
Yes! She Knows She's Here	$15 + $5 /1st copy shipping*	___	__
Nicola Schaefer's NEW Book			
Inclusion: Recent Research	$20 + $5 /1st copy shipping*	___	__
What the Research Says - G.Bunch & A. Valeo			
The All Star Company	$25 + $5 /1st copy shipping	___	__
It's About Building Teams!			
Lessons for Inclusion	$15 + $5 /1st copy shipping	___	__
Curriculum Ideas for Inclusion in Elementary Schools			
Kids, Disabilities & Regular Classrooms	$15 + $5 /1st copy shipping	___	__
Annotated Bibliography of Children's Literature on Disabilies			
What's Really Worth Doing	$12 + $5 /1st copy shipping	___	__
Judith Snow's new Book on Circles			
The Inclusion Papers - Strategies & Stories	$15 + $5 /1st copy shipping	___	__
The Careless Society - John McKnight	$20 + $5 /1st copy shipping	___	__
Who Cares - David Schwartz	$20 + $5 /1st copy shipping	___	__
Changes in Latitudes/Attitudes	$15 + $5 /1st copy shipping	___	__
Petroglyphs - the High School book from UNH	$15 + $5 /1st copy shipping	___	__
Treasures	$15 + $5 /1st copy shipping	___	__
Reflections on Inclusive Education	$12 + $5 /1st copy shipping	___	__
Don't Pass Me By	$12 + $5 /1st copy shipping	___	__
Action for Inclusion Classic on Inclusion	$15 + $5 /1st copy shipping	___	__
Parcours: Path en francais	$15 + $5 /1st copy shipping	___	__
L'Intégration en Action (en Français)	$15 + $5 /1st copy shipping	___	__
From Behind the Piano	$12 + $5 /1st copy shipping	___	__
The Whole Community Catalogue	$15 + $5 /1st copy shipping	___	__
Inclusion – Exclusion Poster (18 X 24)	$10 + $5 /1st copy shipping	___	__
Inclusion News (free with book order)	$2 + $2 for shipping	___	__
Inclusion News in Bulk (box of 150)	$50 – includes shipping in NA	___	__
Path KIT - 2 Videos + Workbook	$115 + $10 shipping per kit	___	__

* Shipping: Books: $5 for 1st+ $2/copy up to 10; Videos: $8 for 1st+ $4/copy up to 5. BULK Rate: 1